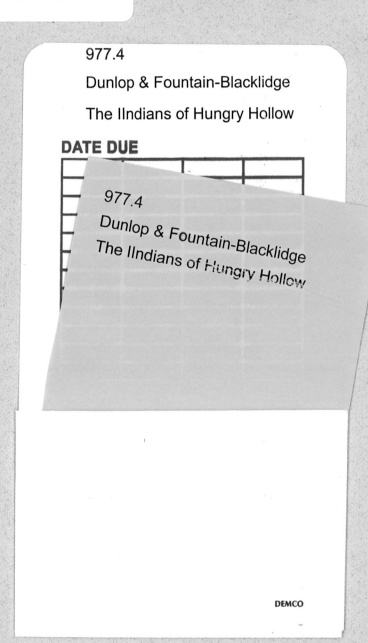

977.4

Dunlop & Fountain-Blacklidge

The IIndians of Hungry Hollow

DATE DUE

977.4

Dunlop & Fountain-Blacklidge

The IIndians of Hungry Hollow

DEMCO

The Indians of Hungry Hollow

The Indians of Hungry Hollow

Bill Dunlop, *Ottawa,*

and

Marcia Fountain-Blacklidge, *Chippewa*

The University of Michigan Press
Ann Arbor

Copyright © by the University of Michigan 2004
All rights reserved
Published in the United States of America by
The University of Michigan Press
Manufactured in the United States of America
♾ Printed on acid-free paper

2007   2006   2005   2004   4   3   2   1

A CIP catalog record for this book is available from the British Library.

Library of Congress Cataloging-in-Publication Data

Dunlop, Bill, 1926–
   The Indians of Hungry Hollow / Bill Dunlop and Marcia Fountain-
Blacklidge.
      p.   cm.
   ISBN 0-472-11115-9 (cloth : acid-free paper) — ISBN 0-472-08653-7
(paper : acid-free paper)
      1. Indians of North America—Michigan—History.   2. Indians of
North America—Michigan—Social life and customs.   I. Fountain-
Blacklidge, Marcia, 1949–   II. Title.

E78.M6 D86   2000
977.4'00497—dc21   99-87885

*This book is dedicated
to the
Indians of Hungry Hollow
and especially
to the very few
who are still alive*

Acknowledgments

The first thing I must tell you is that because I left school at 16 and enlisted in the U.S. Navy during WW II, I can neither type nor do correct punctuation. I write everything in longhand and then have someone do the typing and correct the punctuation.

In 1978, I started doing short stories for the Indian newsletter *Turtle Talk*. Virginia Medacco Herr encouraged me to try my hand at writing despite my lack of training. "A Tribute to Jim Thorpe; The Greatest Athlete Who Ever Lived," was the first story we did together. It went over real well with the Indian people in Grand Rapids. Other articles followed until I was a regular contributor to *Turtle Talk*.

I want to thank all the women at the now defunct Grand Rapids Inter-Tribal Council who typed up my handwritten articles. I also want to thank its former Executive Director, Levi Rickert, and Marcia Barber, former editor of *Turtle Talk*.

Bill Dunlop
Grand Rapids, Michigan
2003

It is impossible to adequately express the gratitude I feel for the love and support provided to me by my family and friends throughout this process. My husband Kent, my daughter Lia, her husband Dexter, my grandchildren Disney and Drake, and friends Marcheta, Lee Ann and Anne have played too important of a role not to mention individually. There are many more friends and family members whose support has been vital to me and whom I would like to individually name but for brevity's sake can not. I believe you know who you are, so please accept my heartfelt appreciation.

Marcia L. Fountain-Blacklidge

Contents

Introduction

In the still of the night, when others are captives of their dreams, she comes to me. Her gentle slopes, tar-papered homes, and many faces dance across my mind, awakening the sounds and sights of a time long past. Hungry Hollow was my first love, and like any true love, our journey together was not always an easy one. I owe much of what I consider to be good in myself to her. My name is Bill Dunlop. My people, the people of Hungry Hollow, are Indian.

Many in Hungry Hollow had roots planted there long before the white man knew about these shores. As Indians, we had a way of life that suited us; at its center were the land upon which we walked and the Creator. After the white man came, much of that changed. When he first came to our land, we accepted his arrival and taught him what we knew so he could survive. We did a pretty good job, because as the years went on, his numbers grew.

Over time, we lost most of our land and found ourselves struggling to fit into what had become his world. Our days of abundance and freedom were gone. The dark times, foretold in our prophecies, were upon us. These were the times into which I was born, the early years of the twentieth century.

Some of our survivors lived on the edge of a small town in northern Michigan. We called our town-within-a-town Hungry Hollow, simply because the name fit. As a young boy, I thought being Indian meant struggling to survive. Now, I am an old man and have learned to see beyond those struggles to a deeper meaning.

Hungry Hollow was more than a geographical location. She was more than a group of impoverished Indians living on the same street. Hungry Hollow was the home of a people, and like our ancestors, we belonged to one another. Our working, playing, and struggling together got us through the hard times.

The story that follows is an opportunity for you to see Hungry Hollow through my eyes. Regardless of what you know about the devastation that has fallen upon Indian people, Hungry Hollow has a different story to tell. She bears witness that the suffering and loss the people of Hungry Hollow endured were not fierce enough to destroy the love and caring they had for each other. Back then, we learned this by living it. Today, we are scattered about like leaves in a storm. Our young ones have few opportunities to experience what I've always taken for granted. I can see young people of every color and nation struggling with the uncertainties and challenges of today's world.

What can be done, you may ask? I did. I could see the problem, but I couldn't see any answers. However, the Creator is patient. He saw my heart and sent me a helper. Marcia Fountain-Blacklidge, a Chippewa, listened to my stories and urged me to write them in a book. At first, I thought she was simply chasing after our brothers the wild geese. When a season passed and the idea remained, I began to rethink my position. After many prayerful horizons, I became convinced her idea was a good one. However, I am an oral storyteller and will remain one. Marcia is a writer. Together, we have given new life to the Indians of Hungry Hollow. It is my prayer their story will teach you that the worth of a people can be measured not by what they have accumulated but only by how they treat one another.

Storytellers help a people to see and remember their true nature. We Indians have always believed one must know where he has been before he can know who he is and where he is going. We also believe everyone has something to give. These stories, the story of Hungry Hollow, Marcia and I humbly offer as our part, our gift to all people and to their journey. May it serve you well and may your eyes be opened to your true self, each and every one of you. Megwetch. That is, thank you.

· 1 ·

Boxcar Blues

My heart went out to that little girl. She was standing in the boxcar door holding onto her father's pant leg. Her hair was windblown, and her face was dirty from the black soot of the steam engine. She was barefoot, because her kind of child wears shoes only in winter. Her only clothing was a shift, a crude dress made of flour sacking.

These were the times the white man would come to call the heart of our country's Great Depression, a time when all of America was down for the count. Cigarettes were 7 cents a pack; gasoline was 8 cents a gallon; a loaf of bread cost 9 cents; and a spaghetti dinner cost 17 cents. The trouble was, where was one to get the 17 cents?

There was no welfare, no social security, and no dole of any kind. Work was as scarce as hens' teeth, and if one didn't work, one didn't eat. In Hungry Hollow, we missed more meals than most. We were the last hired and the first fired. We were Indian.

The tar-papered houses tucked side by side up Sheridan Street looked scarred and frail in the strong summer light.

Could we make it through another winter?

Suddenly, I didn't want to think anymore. I was standing smack-dab in the middle of early summer and as close to heaven on earth as you can get. I took a deep breath and let Petoskey's blue sky, fresh air, and 78-degree temperature wash over me. I needed it. I'd just spent the better part of the afternoon scouring the city dump looking for bottles with caps. As strange as it may sound, I was glad to do it.

It all started when school let out that year. We would stand along Bear River where the Pennsylvania Railroad crossed the lower end of Hungry Hollow and watch the trains. We called ourselves "the Sheridan Street Rats." Flop, Oakley, Sparky, Hermes, Ralph,

Joe, Archie, Smokey, and I had come up with that name for a ball tournament we'd entered, and it stuck.

"I'll bet it's a flyer," Flop called out.

The vibration of metal on metal wiggling into our feet had signaled a train was approaching.

"Naw," Oakley shouted while covering his ears. "Too light for a flyer. If it was, she'd be rattling our teeth by now."

The big black circle of a fast freight burst onto the horizon, screaming her warning as she went. Flop's guess was close. Fast freights and flyers did sound alike. The difference was in their engines. Two-engine trains were known as "flyers." Their loud warning whistle always caused a ruckus in the small towns or villages they sped through without stopping. Those places were soon dubbed "whistle-stops." Fast freights had only one engine, and although not quite as fast as flyers, they, too, blew through those places. Slow freights were a different story. They stopped everywhere they could.

As usual, Oakley was right. We didn't mind, though. He had a knack for being able to do whatever he made up his mind to accomplish. Smart as a whip, he paid attention to things most people didn't even notice. Painting and drawing came easily to him. Music was another one of his specialties. When Oakley was around, you could usually count on something good happening. I guess that's why folks liked him so much. I know I did—and would have even if he weren't my cousin.

As far as predicting trains, Oakley had an edge. Freight trains always outnumbered the passenger ones. In those days, trains were the most plentiful thing going. That's how things and people generally got around. Roads and highways were unpaved and scarce. If all you got from using them was a headache, you were lucky.

Everyone preferred to travel by train. Some bought tickets, while many others "rode the rails."

That's what everyone called it. Everyone did it, even though it was against railroad rules.

Day after day unnamed faces passed through on boxcars, flat-cars, and coal gondolas. A few of the heartier souls even rode the tops of those things. They crisscrossed the country going hither and yon and back and forth. They'd hear about fruit needing to be picked two states away or a canning factory needing labor somewhere else. With little more than a rumor on which to hang their hopes, they'd pick up and head to the nearest freight yard. The place didn't matter. The slightest hope of finding a job did.

Riding the rails, especially the boarding part, was dangerous. However, as the Depression deepened, so did everyone's desperation. It wasn't long before families could be seen standing in the freight-car doors. They'd risked a lot to be there. Because of the women and children, their only chance to board came when freights stopped for coal. These were also the times the railroad men had the best chance of catching illegal riders. Grown men and boys had more options. They could catch trains "on the fly." You'd see them run as fast as they could alongside the moving train, reach up and grab a rung on one of the railcar ladders, and pull themselves up. Occasionally, you'd spot someone running alongside and grabbing the hasp of the boxcar door. This was even more dangerous, because if they lost their grip and let go, they ended up under the boxcar, where the wheels got them. Whenever we saw a one-legged hobo, we knew what had happened. We also knew he'd been lucky.

Dressed in ragged and torn clothes, rail riders were dirty from head to foot. Dirty not because they didn't care to wash, but because of the soot and black smoke the steam engines belched out. Each locomotive engine came by its nickname "dirty face" honestly.

Occasionally, trains would require repair en route. During those downtimes, we would strike up conversations with the passengers. We talked to one man who was taking his entire family to a place in Indiana where tomatoes were canned. At least this was what he'd heard. He'd also heard they had a camp there for workers. They could live rent-free in little shacks while they canned tomatoes. It was heaven-sent for a man with a family.

Rail riders stayed hungry and thirsty. They were the illegal cargo. The legitimate stuff didn't need food or water. No one had to tell us those people were suffering. It was written all over their faces.

At first, I tried to catch their eyes so I could send them a smile of encouragement. It didn't work. I soon found out misery has a way of clinging to those who watch it. The trouble was, none of us knew what to do about it. Not even Oakley.

One morning, my father joined Flop and me on the back stoop. He had his usual cup of hot tea in hand.

"I heard there might be some work at the Michigan Maple this summer."

I watched the steam roll from his cup as his blowing cooled its contents.

"That's not to say I'll get hired. No telling how many men it'll draw."

He took a small sip, only to find it too hot. He resumed blowing.

"I've noticed you boys down near the river a lot lately. What's the draw?"

He took another sip and found the temperature to his liking.

"Nothin' much. Just watchin' the freights and flyers," Flop told him.

"Seems like there's more and more people on those trains everyday," I added.

My father nodded.

As those soot-covered faces and blank stares filled my head, I blurted out, "I don't know how they stand it."

The force of my words startled all three of us.

My dad stood up and took another drink from his cup.

He put his hand on my shoulder, gave it a squeeze, and then handed me his cup.

"You boys stick close to home 'til I get back."

Waiting is never easy, and that morning our curiosity made it worse. After what seemed like an eternity, we spotted him at the bottom of the hill carrying something red.

"Bill," he shouted out, "run and get my tools."

When I returned, I found Flop and him inspecting the wheels and the handle of what had been a wagon. He told us what he wanted done to it and then disappeared again!

We busied ourselves fixing the wagon and then testing it out. As the morning wore on, the rest of our pack joined us.

"He's back," Sparky called out. "And he's carrying something, but I can't make out what it is."

We rushed to meet him. The mysterious object turned out to be a large, empty, cardboard box. We were still puzzling over this as he fixed it to the wagon.

"It's up to you now," he said. "Go to the dump and bring back all the bottles you can find. This little wagon ought to carry quite a few."

We grabbed the handle of the wagon and headed towards the dump to do as we were told. Each of us was pushing and shoving trying to be the one to pull the wagon.

"Take it easy, boys," my father shouted after us.

Then he added, "Be sure all the ones you bring back have caps!"

It didn't take us long to reach our destination. We scoured every inch of that dump! To look at us you would have thought we were digging for gold. It wasn't long before our wagon was piled high with bottles. Triumphantly, we returned home! The clanging and rattling of our cargo was enough to pull several neighbors from their houses.

"What you boys gonna do with all those bottles?" they wanted to know.

My father stood in our front yard with his hands on his hips and a big grin across his face. He helped us unload the bottles and then taught us how to carefully wash and rinse them.

"Pay attention," he warned. "No use doin' it at all if you don't do it right."

Hungry Hollow didn't have a city water supply. We didn't have a sewer system either. What we did have were four good water wells. Pure, clear water bubbled from the sandy bottoms fed by natural springs. We filled every bottle.

We were a different bunch of kids who went down to the railroad that afternoon. With our cargo beside us and my father supervising, we tossed bottle after bottle of water to the people on the passing trains.

Oakley and I worked side by side all afternoon. As early evening approached, one more boxcar came rattling down the tracks. I knew this one carried a family, because I could make out a man and a child in the doorway. As it got closer, I could see the child was a little girl. She was standing in the boxcar door holding on to her father's pant leg.

Oakley handed two bottles of water up to her father, and something in me forced my eyes to find hers. She smiled and waved. I felt my heart melt all the way to my toes. Her whole family started waving and calling out thank-you after thank-you. My arm flew into the air, shouting back the biggest "You're welcome!" it could muster. Oakley's arm did the same. We didn't stop until they were well out of sight.

I've thought of her from time to time. I'd get to wondering if things were ever going to get better and then she'd pop into my head.

Once in awhile I'd ask my sister, Muggs, who knew just about everything, "Will it ever get better?"

She'd tell me, "Good things will come to us, we'll just have to wait."

Deep down inside I'd wonder if Muggs was right. I was afraid waiting was all we'd ever do. I'd wonder what kind of answers that little girl's daddy gave her and if those answers satisfied her any more than the ones I got did me. She had to feel choked by the same poverty that had its hand around my neck.

I'd close my eyes and see her lying on the floor of a boxcar rumbling and rattling through the night. Her hands were clutching an empty belly and her eyes were shut tight. She was trying her best to squeeze out all that pain and escape into her dreams.

I hope she made it. I hope her family got where they were going safe and sound. I hope her daddy found work. And most of all, I hope he replaced that flour sack with the prettiest dress money could buy and bought her shoes long before it got cold.

Springwater was all we had to share with those railroad riders. Discarded bottles with caps and hard work were our only means of sharing it. We heard many a shouted "Thank you!" and "God bless you!" as the trains rolled down the tracks.

We took a lot of bottles from the dump that summer. We left a lot of misery as payment.

Indian Barber Shop

The summer sun was peaking over Little Traverse Bay as Flop and I raced out the back door. Slam! Bang! Once again we'd forgotten our mother's cardinal rule: No door slamming! We stopped long enough to hear if we would be called back. One second then two passed without a sound, and we took off running. Our destination: Bear River. Our mission: to collect wild onions to flavor my mother's fish-head soup. Its ingredients included the fishheads that were thrown out the back of the fish markets. These heads were considered garbage by the moneyed white folks. Her tasty soup proved them wrong each time she made it.

Cracked corn was another diet staple. It was actually dried field corn cracked into small pieces and then sold as chicken feed. It only cost pennies a pound. We soaked it in water and salt for hours to make it soft and then added a little meat. The problem with this soup was that meat was so hard to come by.

Flop and I made our way through the grass and other plants hugging the riverbank. Porcupine, fox, opossum, and raccoon had left their signature for those who knew where to look. Most people didn't. They'd walk over them in their hurry to throw a fishing line in the water, or they'd erase them by laying down a blanket for a picnic. We knew better.

With practice, tracking had gotten much easier for us. Hunting had not. Game wardens had become unbending in their enforcement of hunting seasons and game limits. The increasing numbers of unskilled but well-armed hunters were threatening to destroy the wildlife and themselves. It was anyone's guess as to which would go first. The government decided the sale of hunting licenses would help the enforcement side of the situation. If you were caught hunting without a license, you could count on going to jail. Every man in Hungry Hollow needed to hunt, but not one of them could afford the required license. Not one of them could afford to spend time in jail for trying to feed their families. Hard times bring hard choices.

That's how old Bill Dunlop and his two boys became beloved. William Dunlop, Sr., was by far the best hunter and tracker in the woods of northern Michigan. Even he had many close calls with the game warden, but he didn't let those get in his way. He was determined they never would. He even set about teaching his two sons all he knew. Before long, we were hunting for everyone in Hungry Hollow who couldn't hunt for themselves. We kept a back room of our house filled with as much game meat as we could. Visitors seeking meat came to our back door under the cover of night. My father never asked for payment of any kind for the meat he passed out. Those who could brought a few things to share. It was not unusual to get up in the morning and find a few potatoes, some beans, carrots, or a head of cabbage sitting on our kitchen table, which had been empty the night before. Once, someone left five 12-gauge shotgun shells. I especially liked it when Mrs. Sogot left a pan of corn bread. Tears came to my mother's eyes one morning when she found a pair of hand-knitted mittens. They were very pretty.

It was not uncommon for people to put in special requests to my father. Uncle Ike, my mother's uncle, asked for rabbit. Waboose seemed to be his favorite meat. Old Seezon wanted porcupine. She could make it taste like roast beef, although none of us knew how she did it. Old Sam wanted pancreas meat, which we called the "lights" of the deer. The women turned the porcupine quills into beautiful baskets that they then sold. They used the money for things they couldn't make themselves, like salt, pepper, and baking powder. No part of the animal was wasted. Neither were my father's efforts. Before long, it was clear one of his sons would follow in his footsteps.

My brother, Flop, could do things in the woods I've never seen done by any other man. For instance, he could mark a tree and walk a half-mile circle back to that same tree. The particular woods or tree didn't matter to Flop. He was as at home in the woods as you or I would be in our own living room.

That morning our "quarry" was wild onions. However, we couldn't resist checking out the calling cards that'd been left by other visitors to the river. We'd been keeping a close eye on one deer herd in particular since early spring. Flop was the first to spot their tracks that morning.

"Bill," he called, motioning to me. "They've been here, but I don't like what I see."

He dropped to his knees to examine a milkweed pod.

"Will you look at all these dewclaws!" I exclaimed.

Flop, now intently sniffing the pod, said nothing. There was a maze of deer tracks sprawled all over the ground. I could make sense out of some of them. The widest and deepest dewclaws belonged to bucks, while the narrower, more shallow ones were those of does. The fawns' tracks were the shallowest. We knew a lot about this herd. Summer had been good to them. Their tracks had grown in size and depth. Occasionally, two new sets would appear. This meant fawns had been born on other days, the tracks told us that the young bucks had been at each other and were testing the dominance of their elders.

Less skilled than Flop, I was soon bored. I also knew those leeks weren't going to get into that fishhead soup by themselves.

"Bill."

"What?"

"Somethin's happened to that big doe with the new fawns. It's got the whole herd twitchy."

"What do ya mean?"

I bent over for a closer look.

"Look. The fawns' tracks are scrambling every which way and then back again."

"So? Maybe they just felt frisky."

"No. The herd is closed in too tight for that. They should be glued to their mother."

"OK. Maybe they got separated from her and were scrambling to get to her."

"Yea, except for one thing."

"What's that?"

"Her tracks aren't here."

I took another look, and this time I saw it too. Clear as day.

"By golly, you're right!"

Once again I'd been caught just looking at tracks while Flop was busy reading the story they had to tell.

"Bill?" Flop said, telegraphing the rest of his question with his face.

"Oh, go on. I'll get the leeks and see you back at the house later. Don't be late again for supper, or Mom will have both our hides."

"Don't worry."

He scurried off to solve the mystery of the missing doe.

At the edge of the tree line he turned and shouted, "Thanks, Bill. I owe you."

"Aw, go on," I called back as he disappeared into the woods.

I didn't mind getting the leeks. The river was a great companion. Its smooth flowing current set a nice work pace. My thoughts were soon drifting along in an easy here-and-there rhythm as my hands dug in the moist soil.

Without warning, Frank Greenleaf popped into my head. The story of the great rescue of 1908 was today. Not in any way was I going to miss that! A quick count of my work told me I could head home.

Frank Greenleaf was the "haircutter" for all the Indians of Hungry Hollow. Notice I didn't say "barber." There is a difference. Barbers do facials, steam treatments, manicures, and eyebrow trims and are licensed by the state. Frank Greenleaf didn't have a state license, but he did cut hair. He had one service and one fee. His price was firm, but if you didn't have the five cents, he'd cut your hair anyhow. Frank trusted his customers to keep track of what they owed him and to pay him when they could. To my knowledge, no one ever let him down.

His place of haircutting was on his enclosed back porch. People gathered on that porch to do more than get their hair cut. Frank had a small celluloid table radio, which ran on electricity. It was the only radio in all of Hungry Hollow, and Frank's house had the only electricity. The radio was often the center of attention. The men liked to listen to the news. They especially liked the sports news, because we Indians were so very proud of Jim Thorpe. We were always eager to hear about his accomplishments. Sometimes Frank would let us kids listen to the tales of Jack Armstrong, the All-American Boy, or to the adventures of Flash Gordon. Sunday afternoons were especially fun. We would join Tennessee Jed in his adventures, then go to the Inner Sanctum, and finally be scared out of our wits by the Shadow. Breathless and trembling, we would head home glad to have a whole week between ourselves and our next encounter with that scary figure.

Frank's radio wasn't the only draw to his back porch. You could often run into relatives or friends you hadn't seen in awhile and catch up on visiting. World and community news and events were discussed and even argued there on a regular basis. These were times for the adults to talk and the children to listen.

We would sit cross-legged and pay full attention. Every now and then, old Frank Michigan or Paul Day-Bird would turn to us and say, "What do you boys think of that?"

A torrent of words would explode forth. Our fathers couldn't tell us to be quiet then or shoot looks of warning our way. A wise man had given us permission to speak! We never failed to take full advantage of that opportunity and would ask question after question.

The elders liked to gather at Frank's to tell stories. They never had to worry about attracting an audience. Their stories were every bit as good as the radio adventures of the Lone Ranger or Hopalong Cassidy.

As I made my way home, a glance towards Frank's told me folks were already gathering. I broke into a run.

Exactly one week had passed since Isaac Naska had mentioned

the great rescue. We boys had begged him to tell us more, but he'd refused.

"Patience, grandsons. I'm an old man and too tired to give such a story everything it deserves today. My next visit will be soon enough."

Then he smiled and settled back in his chair. "Turn on that talking box, Frank. It must be time for that jumping horseman to ride again."

Those words brought forth the very response he'd hoped for.

"Hopalong Cassidy, Grandfather!" we shouted in unison.

"Yes, yes. That's right. I'm happy to have such smart grandsons. It does my heart good."

Out of breath, I burst through our back door and thrust the leeks into my mother's lap.

"Where's Francis?" she wanted to know as she wrapped her apron around the leeks.

"Out chasing deer."

"Out chasing deer?" she began, but I was already rounding the corner of our house on my way to Frank's.

"No time to talk. Don't want to miss the great rescue of 1908!"

There was standing room only when I opened Frank's creaky porch door. A quick scan of the crowd told me I could relax. Oakley had saved a spot for me right in front.

Isaac Naska sat in the center of the elder's row with both hands propped on his cane. On his left sat Paul Day-Bird, ready to add details when necessary. Frank Michigan sat on Isaac's right, ready to contribute as well.

The room was buzzing with friendly chatter. I gingerly stepped between legs and feet to take my seat as I returned Oakley's hello smile.

That Oakley. Darned if he didn't know to save only one space. It's not like Flop to miss one of these sessions. How the heck does Oakley do that?

Isaac cleared his throat. He was ready to begin. Silence rippled through the room until you could've heard a pin drop.

"Good morning," he began. "As I recall, it was in the moon of the ripe berries that the lake got in one of the worst moods ever known in these parts."

Paul and Frank nodded their agreement.

"Of course, you wouldn't have known that by looking at the daybreak sky. Only the wave readers knew what the lake had in store for us. We relied upon them to keep us safe when we fished or traveled on the water. For several days running they'd warned us a storm was brewing. They told us travel on the lake too close to its arrival could prove deadly. Unfortunately, not everyone had the benefit of such wise counsel.

"The storm broke that day, just as the wave readers had predicted. It showed no mercy as it pounded wind and rain onto everything within its reach. It whipped the lake into a frenzy. The waves got as tall as mountains and as wild as a rabid animal. Trees were snapping and falling everywhere. Debris was flying every which way, spewing fear among onlookers as it went. In the midst of all this terror, one man went out to gauge the storm. His name was Kenoshmeg, and he was the first to spot them."

"Yes," agreed Frank Michigan. "He was at the highest place on the tallest hill above Waganagaisk. That is what we called it then, the place of the crooked tree. Today this place is called Good Hart."

There was a general exclamation of understanding. I knew this very place! I'd been there with my father. I might have even stood on the very same spot as Kenoshmeg!

Isaac continued. "Wiping the rain from his eyes while trying to ignore the wind biting through his clothes, Kenoshmeg fought to see the lake. When he finally succeeded, he could hardly believe what bobbed on the horizon. It was a small boat in big trouble! Being a fisherman, he knew you turned your boat into the wind in a storm, not sideways. Any ship captain would know to do the same.

"Mik-sa-be came up behind Kenoshmeg. He too quickly understood the situation. Together they hurried down to alert the other Indians.

"Aboard the yacht, three men were in mortal fear of their lives.

Their motor had quit, and they had no steering. They'd played out their anchor to its full length, but the water was too deep and the anchor had nothing to hold it. They were doing the only thing they could. They were praying loud and hard. In all that ruckus, they had no way of knowing that many Indians had gathered on the beach and on the tall hills of Good Hart. The Indians were watching, praying, and trying their best to figure a way to rescue these men. Everyone knew these strangers would die if their vessel broke up. No one believed their vessel could hold up through the whole storm.

"Concern for these mens' lives filled the hearts and minds of the Indians, but the idea of saving them produced as much concern for any potential rescuers. With only rowboats and muscles to use in such an attempt, who could blame them?

"The storm continued unabated the rest of the day. As the light faded, Ben Batose, who was on the high bluffs, could still see the boat tossing and writhing in between the waves. The Indians on the beach built a huge fire and kept vigil all through the night. A few Indians did the same on the high bluffs. They wanted whoever was on the storm-tossed boat to catch sight of the fires and take hope.

"No rescue attempt could be made in the dark of night. Morning would bring the first opportunity for action. No one knew if the strangers' boat could hold together that long.

"As each minute crept by, the storm raged on. The women kept food and hot tea and coffee available at the Kiogima home. The men, mostly fishermen and farmers, laid plans.

"Almost all volunteered to try the rescue, but there were two who stood out. Joseph Okenotego and Joseph Kadabinesse were the brawniest and best rowers. Kadabinesse owned the best boat. They would make the attempt.

"The wind was still shrieking and tearing everything in sight when morning dawned. Now even more people gathered on the beach and on the bluffs. Every face strained towards the boat, but only the white tops of huge waves came into view. As it got lighter, great shouts went up! First from the Indians on the bluffs, and then from those on the beach. The boat had made it through the night.

Better yet, the Indians knew the anchor had caught, for the boat now faced directly into the storm. Best of all, it was only a half-mile from shore.

"Kadabinesse's boat was dragged to the edge of the beach. Agonizing minutes dragged by while the two watched and waited for a break in the waves. Minutes turned into hours while the storm stubbornly kept the lake too wild to enter. The Indians knew the cruiser couldn't last another night. No one spoke of what that meant for its three passengers. Finally, the two Josephs pushed their boat into the lake. No one had urged them to do this. Everyone knew this was a matter to be decided only by them. Once the remaining Indians saw that a decision had been reached, they did their best to support and aid them by cheering and shouting encouragement.

"The storm strained and worked the two rowers' every muscle. Over and over, their meager progress was thwarted as their boat was tossed sideways or back towards the shore.

"Those on shore now feared for the lives of all five men. They could only wonder how long the rescuers' efforts could continue.

"In the boat, the two Josephs were wondering the same thing. The strain showed in their faces as they gasped for breath between assaulting waves. Pelting rain made even squinting difficult and speech impossible. Besides, talking would have taken too much energy.

"Somehow, the two managed to work as one. They dug in and found reserves they never knew existed. Pulling on those oars became all that mattered as they aimed for the disabled boat, fighting wind and water every inch of the way.

"As they were tossed onto the crest of one wave and then dashed into the deepest trough of the next, the uncertainty of their fate tugged on their resolve. They disappeared and reappeared time and again. All hearts back on shore and in the cruiser beat with wild abandon.

"Some of the women had gathered around the beach fire. They knelt and fervently prayed the Rosary, beseeching the Blessed Mother to bring all her children safely to shore. On the highest bluff, the men around the fire began to sing a song of tribute to bravery. On his drum, Kenoshmeg's strong hands gave voice to the heartbeat of his people. It filled the tired muscles of Okenotego and Kadabinesse with new and much-needed strength.

"Rowing was not the only challenge these men faced. Many times their boat was almost swamped by the heavy breakers. They would lose precious ground as they scrambled to bail the intruding water. All the while, the steady drumming of the heartbeat of the people called out to them from their faithful supporters on shore. Fortunately, these two had the ears to hear this above the storm and over their own fears.

"Finally, their boat bumped against the lee hull of the yacht. The stranded men were pale and weak from their ordeal. Kadabinesse grabbed the edge of their boat and held on for all he was worth. Seeing the size of the rescue boat filled the men with uncertainty, and they refused to move. Okenotego began to coax them to at least try the transfer. The first man to respond to Okenotego's coaxing was not rewarded for his effort. As he got one leg partially into the rowboat, a wave crashed down upon them. Kadabinesse somehow managed to keep his grip, but the stranger was tossed back into his boat. Now the three were more terrified than ever. More coaxing. More yelling. At last the man decided to try again. This time the transfer succeeded! Encouraged by their friend's success, the other two were now ready to try.

"However, the storm was not finished with them. It got even more ferocious. As the second man was transferring, two waves came crashing in, one right after the other. The two boats crashed into each other with a loud crack! Kadabinesse barely had time to pull his hands back before they would have been crushed beyond repair. Just as quickly, the boats were tossed apart and the second stranger was deposited into the water. Okenotego managed to grab a piece of his shirt and held on while they were hit by two more waves. Kadabinesse was forced to bail to keep them afloat, while Okenotego pulled the second stranger to safety. Now the two Josephs had to take to the oars again to get close enough to the other boat to complete the transfers. After several minutes of trying, they reached the boat a second time. Things would not get easier. Kadabinesse grabbed the boat, once again holding on for all he was worth. The third man, now paralyzed with fear, was more reluctant than the other two had been. Okenotego kept at him. His two friends joined Okenotego's efforts. Time and again the waves broke Kadabinesse's hold, throwing everyone into new peril. Finally, the third man relented, and his transfer was complete. All were battered and bruised from their effort; yet they still faced the trip back to shore. To their dismay, Okenotego and Kadabinesse soon found it demanded even more effort than the trip out. The added numbers and weight to the boat required bailing more often and with greater speed.

"The storm breakers and ferocious wind continued as wild and unpredictable as ever, forcing their return journey to take a diagonal direction towards shore. Just ahead, a wall of large and jagged rocks awaited them. If the boat and its precious cargo were swept up and smashed into them, an ugly but certain death would follow.

"Miraculously, fate intervened. A huge wave swept the rowboat up and dumped it and its five passengers some twenty feet onto the beach.

"Great shouts of joy and thanksgiving rang out! The five men were carried to the warmth and safety of the Kiogima home. The storm howled on through the night, but no one took the time amidst the celebration and retelling of the great rescue to pay it much mind. By the first light of dawn, it was over. The lake had belched out debris all over the beach. It was still in upheaval, with huge waves continuing to crash ashore. In one of those strange ironies only nature can conjure up, the cruiser now sat on the beach just beyond the little rescue boat. At first, everyone thought the grand rescue had been for naught. Given a few more hours, the three strangers would have been safely delivered on shore without needing any help. A closer look cast all doubts aside. Yes, the boat had been delivered to shore, but the hole in its hull gave testimony to how near its three occupants came to meeting their maker.

"News of the rescue of William Rout, age 41, Alfred Shampine, age 44, and Amad Lavake, age 31, spread throughout the area. When it got to the right ears, the Carnegie Hero Fund Commission decided to award Okenotego and Kadabinesse its Medal of Valor.

"Okenotego and Kadabinesse were reluctant to accept this fine award. They had acted with no thought of recognition. After much discussion, it was decided that although no award had been sought, no harm could come from accepting the gratitude and accompanying medal. There was a fine ceremony with a grand dinner afterwards. Only when we had returned to life as usual did we learn the most surprising news of all. The honor included a cash award of five hundred dollars! This was more money than anyone in Hungry Hollow had ever seen before or since."

Paul and Frank both nodded their heads in confirmation of this point.

Isaac finished his story by saying, "And that is the famous rescue of 1908. May you remember it to tell to your grandsons."

He closed his eyes and leaned back to take a well-deserved rest. We boys could hardly wait to get outside. The day was still young, and we knew exactly where we wanted to be.

· 3 ·

Changing Times

We raced to Bear River. The cool breeze drifting over her banks was a welcome change from the close quarters of Frank's back porch. Flop was just coming out of the woods.

"Boy, did you miss a great story!" we shouted.

He slapped the side of his head. He'd completely forgotten Isaac's promise.

"The story of the 1908 rescue!" he groaned. "I know it was great. I can see it all over your faces."

"Don't worry," I said. "We'll tell you all about it!"

We sat down to do just that. Sparky started the story. He described the storm and where Kenoshmeg first spotted the strangers in peril. His enthusiasm spread to Hermes, who related the details of the night vigil. Before long, the story had taken on a life of its own. It moved through us, picking one and then another to be Kadabinesse or Okenotego. It made its way into our limbs as we reenacted the rescue by paddling furiously against the wind. It tested our courage as the waves tossed us recklessly about the small rowboat. The story drew everyone into its circle, even Flop. He was only an audience of one, but that didn't matter one whit. An audience of thousands could not have been more thrilled.

Oakley finished the story. "The Carnegie people gave a reward with that medal. I bet you can't guess how much it was."

Flop thought for a moment before replying, "I don't know. Was it $25?"

We all roared with delight at how far he had missed it.

"No, it was $500!!"

"Whaaaaaaat!!! Oh, go on. FIVE HUNDRED DOLLARS?!!! I

CAN'T BELIEVE IT!" Flop said, slapping his hand against his forehead.

"Wow! FIVE HUNDRED DOLLARS! A brand new Willys Overland or Studebaker only costs $250. Can you imagine what we could do with all that money?"

His question went unanswered. Silence fell over our small group. Thoughts of what we could do or how we might spend such a huge sum of money danced and sparkled their way through our imaginations. It was all a part of the magic that only the telling of a good story can bring. It hung in the air like a sweet fragrance until Flop's mood scattered it to the winds.

"Wouldn't ya like to do something that great?" Sparky asked.

"Yea. Sure."

Flop's decided lack of enthusiasm didn't go unnoticed.

Sparky tried again. "Did ya hear what I said? Can ya imagine ever earning that big of a reward?"

"I heard ya," Flop barked back. "Do ya want me to do flips or somethin'?"

Anger flashed across Sparky's face, but before he could take things any further, Hermes spoke up. "Hey, it's about dinnertime. I'll race ya home, Archie!"

He took off running.

Sparky and I did too. I thought everyone was with us until a glance towards the river told me otherwise. Flop was talking to Oakley and pointing in the direction of the woods. I turned back.

To my surprise, Sparky did too.

"Hey, Bill. What's up? Is it me?"

I waved him on. "Naw. Flop's just got a lot on his mind. Go on home and get some dinner. We'll see ya later."

With a shrug of his shoulders, Sparky left.

"It's hard to believe anyone would do such a thing," Flop was saying when I joined them.

"Can you retrace your steps?" Oakley wanted to know.

Flop nodded.

"You two get started, and I'll catch up," Oakley told us.

I didn't know what had upset Flop or what he'd just told Oakley. It was clear they wanted me to be a part of things and that was enough for me. As Flop nodded his agreement for the two of us, we headed into the woods toward the south end of the Russian Swamp. Flop quickly filled me in on what had been troubling him and then began reading the doe's tracks like they were road signs. I was no match for his skills, so I just followed along behind. A knot in my gut was talking to me. I was doing my best not to listen.

Flop was too busy to pay me any mind. Occasionally, he would stop to recheck a track or examine a broken vine or plant. At other places, he'd pick up a broken twig or a small clump of dirt and lift it to his nose. He would carefully rub the item on his hand to get a better look at the condition of the blood clinging to it. At times, it would flake onto his hand, and once it smeared all the way across his palm. This type of tracking is tedious and slow going. Piece by piece, we were unraveling the mystery of what'd happened to that doe.

Meanwhile, that darned knot began squeezing my neck, then worked its way into my shoulders. When we reached a small clearing near the Clarion hardwoods, Flop grabbed my arm. He motioned for me to hit the ground. My eyes searched the countryside but found nothing. I started to get up, but Flop stopped me. He began inching forward with his belly hugging the ground. I did the same.

Not twenty yards ahead, we found her. She'd been mutilated almost beyond recognition. I swallowed hard to keep the contents of my stomach from spewing everywhere. Stunned by the savagery that lay before us, we stood up and stared.

"Bill! Flop!"

We both jumped, even though we recognized Oakley's voice. I turned but could not speak. A long, low whistle escaped his lips when his eyes landed on what had been a doe. Moving ahead of us, he squatted beside her to take a closer look.

Flop and I had dressed plenty of deer. My dad had insisted upon it. From the stalking to the dressing out of the animal and cleanup, he'd schooled us. Never had we seen such a careless and wanton butchering. Starting with the shot that had only maimed and not killed her, it was clear she'd come to a needlessly painful end. The final and unforgivable insult was that much of what could have been edible meat lay rotting on the ground.

A rage overtook Flop. He began kicking and screaming and throwing punches into anything in sight. I'd never seen him so angry. Then, without warning, he took off running.

Hunting out of season. Killing a doe of all things. The topper was, whoever did this had let her suffer and didn't even bother to take all she had to offer. I started after Flop, but Oakley stopped me.

"He needs to get it out. Otherwise his insides would end up in pretty much the same shape as this doe. I'll tell you one thing, though, whoever did this is gonna pay for their stupidity."

"What d'ya mean?" I snapped. "We don't have the first clue who did this and we're not going to!"

Unruffled by my anger, he said, "No matter. Nature has its own ways. You see this?"

His finger led my attention to a large section of the animal that'd been crudely cut out and was missing.

"Look closer and take a whiff."

My feet did not move. I had no intention of getting one inch closer.

Oakley looked up. "Bill, nothing is gonna change her suffering. I don't know whether it was cruelty or just plain ignorance that caused it, but I do know this won't be the last time you'll have to face these things. If you let them, they'll turn you inside out and rob you blind. Is that what you want?"

The unexpected harshness in his voice swept through me like a cold wind. I moved closer and took a small whiff. A vile odor assaulted my nose and I jumped back, gagging. My stomach started wrenching, sending its contents shooting from my mouth. The heaving and spasms continued long after it was empty. I managed to take a few steps away from all the carnage and sank to the ground. I lay back with my eyes closed, trying not to breathe too hard or move too quickly.

After a while, I began to feel like myself again. I opened my eyes and sat up. Oakley was sitting not two feet from me, chewing on a piece of sweet grass. He stood up and, offering me his hand, helped me do the same.

"That odor means she had some kind of sickness. She had it before they ever shot her, and she was already dying. Whoever pulled the trigger didn't do right by her though. Either they didn't know they should finish her off cleanly or didn't care enough to. Some folks sure are hard to figure. One thing for certain, they didn't know how sick she was or they wouldn't have taken any of her meat. The stuff that's missing has to be filled with it. What I can't figure is how their noses missed it."

Then he looked at me with all the sternness Oakley could muster. "You damn well better remember this smell, Bill. You're sure to run across it again, but it won't always be so strong. I can guarantee you that."

He put his arm on my shoulder. "Let's go home. Whoever took that meat got a whole lot more than they bargained for. If they are stupid enough to try to eat it, they'll be lucky if it doesn't kill them."

We took our time going home. Fishhead soup flavored by leeks was waiting for us when we got there. So was Flop.

"Better wash up," Mom directed. "Supper's ready."

I took my place at the table as she ladled a generous portion into my bowl. I sipped the steaming liquid and thought of how many times that soup had made me wish I had meat to eat. Not tonight. Not for many more nights to come.

· 4 ·

A Drowned Man

From the turn of the century, Petoskey had grown by leaps and bounds. The Grand Rapids and Indiana Railroad had a big hand in that growth. Company brochures advertised the health, pleasure, gaming, and fishing benefits of the area. Of course, the railroad wanted to provide the transportation to get there.

In those days, summer heat brought misery to the homes of city dwellers. There was no such thing as air-conditioning. The more affluent solved the problem by escaping to places like the East Side of Petoskey. There they could count on being pampered and refreshed by the breezes off Little Traverse Bay. Summer after summer they came. They built spacious homes overlooking the bay and filled them with all kinds of finery.

In late June, one of the worst heat waves anyone in Petoskey could remember arrived. Daily living became difficult to bear.

In Hungry Hollow, our tar-papered roofs soaked up the heat like sponges, turning our homes into ovens.

Things were not much better on "Pill Hill." Located on a bluff overlooking the east bay side of Petoskey, it housed only wealthy men and their families. Folks in Petoskey had given this neighborhood its nickname a few years earlier. An epidemic of some kind spread through Petoskey like fire. Many people died because medicine was in short supply and expensive. The people on the hill had the money to buy what medicine did exist. Those pills saved their lives and gave their neighborhood a new name. Now, though, the sweltering heat dominated life there too. Tempers were short, and the police had their hands full as altercations broke out all over the city. What the heat started, the cops had to finish. Everyone was suffering and on edge. For once, no amount of money could buy you piece of mind.

The Sheridan Street Rats took to the bay. We spent more and more time swimming off the city's boat dock. Our parents encouraged us because it limited the number of squabbles they had to referee. Besides, they knew we were all good swimmers and that no matter how much we might pick on one another, we'd also look after each other.

One morning, on our way to the dock, Oakley asked, "Say, Bill. How long do you think you can stay underwater?"

"Geez, I don't know. Maybe two minutes."

"Aw, come on," Flop challenged me. "You mean more like a minute."

"I bet I can stay under five minutes," Smokey interjected.

That was all it took. The arguing was on. At the end of the pier, Oakley put an end to it.

"We'll find out exactly who can stay under the water the longest. I'll do the timing," he declared, pulling out the watch his father had just given him.

We all looked at each other and grinned. We'd been had! Like most boys, we had a habit of turning everything we could into a contest of one kind or another. Oakley knew this. He'd been itching to show off the pocket watch his dad had worked long and hard to buy. He'd paid the tidy sum of a whole dollar for it.

Oakley was proud of his gift, but he hadn't said a word about it. Bragging just wasn't Oakley's style. He preferred putting the watch to good use. We all knew about the gift. News travels fast in Indian country, and secrets are few and far between there.

The contest was on! With Oakley as our official timer, we lined up on the end of the dock. Each of us was ready to try our hand at capturing the underwater record.

Everyone had a different strategy. Ralph and Hank felt it best to swim as far as they could before surfacing. Sparky, Flop, and Marshall argued that submerging and then staying in place was the way to go. Smokey wouldn't commit himself to any method. Ag Walker thought he'd wait 'til he was in the water to make up his mind.

· 28 ·

Ralph went first. We stopped arguing and watched the water. Oakley stood with watch in hand, carefully monitoring the time. His eyes traveled back and forth from watch to water. Finally, Ralph burst through the surface, shaking the water off his head.

"One minute, 45 seconds," Oakley called out. "Who's next?"

Hank dove into the bay as Ralph swam to the dock. I knelt down and extended my arm to help Ralph muscle his way out of the water. Flop threw him one of our two towels, and he brushed off enough water to avoid shivering. He dropped the towel on the deck and joined our silent vigil. After a few seconds, Hank broke through the surface, gasping for air.

"One minute, 40 seconds" was Oakley's verdict.

"You've got to be joking," Hank protested as he swam to the dock. "I was sure I was under for at least five minutes!"

When he reached the dock, I knelt down to give him a hand up.

"Are you sure you know how to read that thing?" he challenged.

"One minute, 40 seconds" was the only response he got.

He shrugged off the offer of a towel.

"I don't need that," he scowled as he shook the water from his hair.

He moved close enough to Ralph to ensure that some of the excess water would land on the underwater leader. Ralph stood his ground, unwilling to acknowledge the water landing on his bare chest.

Marshall Nanagoose went next and earned a time of one minute, 55 seconds. Flop followed with a time of one minute, 32 seconds. I decided to go next. I didn't really care about beating Marshall. I just wanted to be in the same ballpark as everyone else.

I took deep breaths until I got dizzy. With one last deep breath, I plunged off the dock. The cold water sucked the warmth from my body at a startling pace. I knew it was going to be cold before I dove in, and I'd tried to prepare my body for it. The surprise that shot through me as I stroked towards the bottom told me I'd failed. I squeezed the panic running through my veins into the pit of my stomach. I had to force myself to continue. Bottom weeds soon brushed my skin, and I grabbed them to help me stay put. The panic broke loose, and I fought back the urge to race to the surface. I tried to count the passing seconds, but my mind kept losing itself in panic. When my lungs felt like they were about to burst, I knew I'd stayed as long as I could. I let go of the weeds and headed for the top.

I broke through the surface to the sound of Oakley's voice, "Two minutes and 10 seconds."

Ag Walker was next. Down he went, but he was gone only a few seconds when he shot back out of the water.

A startled Oakley called out, "Fifteen seconds."

Ag's face told us something was wrong. He started to shout something but, forced to take a breath, inhaled some water. Coughing and gagging, he made his way to the dock.

"What'd you say?" we wanted to know.

"Slow down. We can't understand you."

"There's a dead man down there!" he gasped. "He's tangled up in the weeds."

Shock bolted through our group like lightning. We were speechless.

Oakley put his watch down and dove off the pier. We all followed. Near the bottom, we found a man caught in the bottom weeds. His arms and legs dangled with the movement of the water. There was no doubt about it—he was dead! Chills went through me, sticking to my bones. I felt light-headed and disoriented. Oakley grabbed my elbow and pushed me towards the surface. He signaled for everyone else to do the same.

Scrambling onto the dock, we huddled together with our teeth chattering. We knew what had to be done, but not one of us wanted to do it.

The cops. We'd always kept our distance. That was about to change. The heat in the police station hit us like a blast furnace when we walked through the door. The three officers in the station didn't say a word, but their cold stares, sweat-stained uniforms, and open collars spoke volumes. They stopped what they were doing. Narrowing their eyes, they slowly scrutinized each and every one of us.

Finally, one of them spoke. "Now what could bring the likes of you all the way in here on a day like this?"

Hank tried to answer him. "Well, sir . . . ," he began, and then he swallowed because his voice had cracked. "We were swimming down at the dock and found something we need to report."

The policeman seemed to get pleasure out of Hank's discomfort. He tugged at the top of his pants and straightened his shirt as he walked over to us.

Bending over, he got real close to Hank's face. "Now what could you have found that could possibly interest us?"

In a louder and more demanding tone he said, "Speak up, boy. I don't have all day for this nonsense."

I swear I saw the blood drain from Hank's face. He couldn't move.

"We found a body, sir," he said looking down at his feet. "The body of a dead man."

A roar of laughter greeted Hank's report.

"Ain't that rich, boys," one officer hooted to the other two. "Ain't it grand of these boys to be out doing our job for us. Did it so well, they even found a body for us to investigate."

Another round of laughter erupted.

"Now go on!" the officer snarled, breaking off his laughter. "You've had your joke. Get the heck out of here before we decide you need to stay."

A second officer joined in. "That's right. Don't you boys know it's too damn hot to be worrying us with this nonsense? Do like you're told, now, and git!"

I was ready, and I wasn't alone. We all moved towards the door. All of us, that is, except Oakley. He didn't budge.

Moving in front of him, the officer hollered into Oakley's face, "Maybe you don't hear as good as your buddies. I said git!"

Oakley didn't move a muscle.

Looking directly into the policeman's eyes, he said quietly, "We're not playing tricks. We did come across a body."

The policeman took a deep breath, crossed his arms, and glared.

Officer Russ Johnson's entrance broke up the confrontation. A puzzled look came over his face as he started towards the chief's desk.

"What the heck is this convention all about?" he wanted to know.

Maybe it was the soft tone in his voice or maybe we were just hoping he meant what he said, but we rushed to surround him. Everyone started talking at once.

"Hold on, hold on!" he said. "One at time. You don't have to break my eardrums to get my attention."

This time I spoke up. I told him where we'd been swimming, about our contest, and, finally, about Ag's discovery. When I finished, there was dead silence in the station.

"If I give you a rope, can you tie it to the man's leg or arm?" Russ asked.

Our shouts of joy and mass exit towards the dock answered him.

Russ followed us outside and hollered, "Hold it, hold it! Let's all go to the dock together. Go and wait by my car while I get what we need."

He disappeared into the station and returned carrying a rope. We piled into his police car and headed for the dock.

Ag and I swam the rope down. We tied one end to the dead man's leg. Oakley and the others went down to cut the weeds around his body. Ag swam the free end of the rope to the surface and put it in Russ's outstretched hand. We pulled ourselves from the water and got ready to pull the body to the surface.

"Hold on just a minute," Russ said. "Let's do a count to make sure everyone is up. We sure as heck don't need more than one dead body around here."

News of a death spreads like a wildfire in a small town. There are always folks who have the time to stop what they are doing and check out the action. As we did the count Russ requested, we noticed a crowd had gathered at the end of the pier. Among them were several of the most skeptical of Russ's fellow officers. They were hoping to have a good laugh. Listening to a bunch of no-account Indian kids was a foolish waste of Russ's time according to their way of thinking. They didn't want to miss one second of this golden opportunity to heckle and ridicule him.

"Say, Russ, how you gonna use that tire you're getting ready to pull up?" they shouted.

"It's too hot to be weeding the bottom of the bay!" they roared as the cut weeds surfaced.

On and on they went. Russ paid them no mind. He just kept on task.

"All present and accounted for," Oakley reported.

"Good. Now let's get started. Mind you—take it easy. We don't want any pinched hands or feet to add to our trouble."

As the heckling officers continued, we couldn't help but look their way. Russ didn't want our efforts sidetracked.

"Don't pay them any attention. Just keep your eyes and minds on our work," he told us in a stern voice.

We spread out in a small line on the dock, with each of us gripping a section of the rope.

"On count, now," Russ called out. "Ready, one, two, three, and pull!"

We did, and we felt the body tug back at us with equal determination.

"Again," Russ called out. "Ready, pulllllllll!"

Again, we did as we were told. This time we felt a little give on the other end.

"Once more," Russ called out. "Ready, pullllllllllllll!"

This time we felt the body give way. We stopped pulling so hard and waited for the body to float to the surface. We continued to guide it by passing the slack rope slowly through our hands. Russ got behind us and began winding the loose end of the rope around his elbow and shoulder. A gasp spread over the crowd when the body popped up on the surface.

In an instant, Russ's fellow officers were on the end of the dock. They began pushing us out of the way.

"Go on!" one snarled at us. "Get back to where you belong. This is official police business."

"Not so fast," Russ interrupted him. "Okay, boys, you can go on home now. I want you to know you did the right thing and that no man could have asked for better help than what you gave me today."

We nodded and walked off the dock with our heads held high.

"Boys!" he called out.

We turned to look at him.

"Thanks. I just wanted to say thanks."

"You're welcome!" we called back.

There's a lot to be said about the pleasure one gets from doing the right thing.

The police did their job by thoroughly investigating the death of the man we'd discovered. He was a "resorter" who'd fallen overboard from his yacht. No one had reported him missing because his family wasn't due to arrive until several days after we found him. The police ruled his death an accidental drowning.

After that, when things were lost in the waters of that area, we were the first ones summoned. The Sheridan Street Rats had tasted respect, and we liked it!

· 5 ·

Undying Love and
Summertime Blues

The Great Spirit blessed northern Michigan with thick forests and an abundance of clear, beautiful lakes. The elders who congregated on Frank Greenleaf's back porch spoke often of our earlier relations. We called ourselves the *Anishnabeg*, which loosely means "the people." Within the Anishnabeg there were three distinct groups. These were the Ottawa, Potawatomi, and Ojibway, sometimes called Chippewa.

Frank Michigan referred to the Anishnabeg as one large family. They used birch and willow trees to construct their lodges. They hunted in the forests and fished in the lakes. As the United States grew and prospered, so did its demand for quality lumber. Logging camps became a way for Indian men to make a living. They would leave home in late fall and spend the winter in camp cutting timber. The money they earned helped their families to survive. There was a downside. It was very dangerous work.

An Indian, Joe Suchoh, was working as a lumberjack on Beaver Island when a pile of logs that had broken loose trapped him. He nearly lost his life, and both of his legs were broken in several places. He returned to Petoskey to recover. The lumber company doctors did what they could for him, but his legs remained disfigured. The closest he ever came to being able to walk again was to hobble along on crutches.

His accident had dealt Joe a tough hand. The Creator gave him a wonderful and heart-lifting way to play it. Joe often said he was the luckiest man on Mother Earth because of the friend the

Creator brought to keep him company. His friend turned out to be so true and loyal that nothing in life or death could separate them.

His friend's name was Jim-ta-gu, or "Bad Stick." He was a German shepherd and redbone hound mixture. Most people called him a mutt.

Joe fed his dog with meat scraps given to him out the back door of Crago's Economy Market. If Joe got a hot dog, he quickly tore it in half and gave Jim-ta-gu his share. Joe was given a small pension for being crippled, so this was how he and his dog lived.

I liked to visit Joe and Jim-ta-gu. After supper, when things quieted down, I would walk to their house.

Joe would see me coming and would call out, "Good evening, Bill. Did you have yourself a nice day?"

By this time I'd be at his porch. But before I could answer, Jim-ta-gu would be there to greet me. When I say "greet," that is exactly what I mean. Jim-ta-gu would sit up and offer his paw to me. Then he would do just what Joe had taught him. He would "shake hands" with me.

"That's right," Joe would praise him. "You can never be too proper, Jim, when someone comes to call."

Jim would always bark as if he agreed with what Joe was saying. His agreement would make Joe and me have a good laugh.

One evening I got to wondering how Joe and Jim got hooked up together.

"Say, Joe," I asked, "how'd you and Jim get together?"

"Now that's a tale worth telling," he said. "I consider that day the luckiest day of my whole life.

"It wasn't too long after I got up on crutches and began making my way around that I decided it was time to go for a walk. I was still feeling pretty sorry for myself. I'd spent a lot of time remembering how easy walking used to be. I'll tell ya, Bill. Don't ever take those legs the Creator gave you for granted. I did for sure. Fact is, I probably took a lot of chances that, looking back on things, I'd never take today. Getting back to Jim here, I was spending more and more time feeling down and out. I knew my chances for being a family man were gone. I thought all I had to look forward to was a whole lot of pain and one lonely day after the next. I don't think I've ever been so scared.

"I noticed that when I got out and got walking, I felt better. So I did more and more of it. I was hobbling along the railroad tracks one day when I came face-to-face with Jim. I hadn't met up with a dog while I was on my crutches, so I was a bit taken back. I looked straight at him. He looked right back at me. I could see he wasn't much more than a pup. That made me relax some. It was Jim who made the first move though. He just trotted up to me and began licking my pant leg! After such a friendly greeting, I bent over a little to pet him. Then he licked my hand! I knew right away we were going to be good friends. His name came to me right off.

"I called out, 'How do you do Mister Jim-ta-gu? Let's go home.'

"I turned around and started making my way back home. He turned around and followed right behind me. He's never left my side since."

The evening light was still holding when Joe suggested, "Let's head down to the river for a little game of fetch."

Jim raced out of the yard towards the river. Joe and I followed.

"See if you can find a couple of good-size sticks," Joe called out.

I did and handed them to him.

Jim was wagging his tail and jumping around in anticipation of what was coming next. Balancing himself on one crutch, Joe took one of the sticks and threw it as hard as he could into the river.

Jim was off like a shot. Within a few seconds, he'd swum to the stick, had got it in his mouth, and was swimming back to shore.

Once on shore, he ran to Joe and dropped the stick in his waiting hand. With his package delivered, he proceeded to shake the river water off himself at a furious pace. Both Joe and I hollered as the water flew all over us. We didn't really mind, though. Time and again we played out this game, until the evening light was gone.

I said good night to Jim and Joe and headed home. They definitely were good friends and good company.

Everybody liked these two, from the mayor to the street sweeper. And all waved a greeting to them as they passed.

Jim-ta-gu growled at me only once. I was walking through the park that day. I noticed Joe on one of the benches and Jim sitting right beside him. I decided to go over and visit with them. I only got within 20 feet when Jim let out that growl. It not only surprised me but hurt my feelings. I started to say something to Joe about Jim's growling when I heard Joe snore. Then I understood. They often took long walks. On this particular walk, Joe's legs got too tired to finish. He found a park bench to rest on for awhile. He did such a good job of resting that he fell asleep. That's where Jim came in. He wasn't about to let anyone disturb his friend's much needed rest. I noticed that Jim was wagging his tail while he continued to give me that low growl.

If he could have talked, he would have said, "Sorry, I'm only doing my job. Please don't go near Joe until he wakes up. Don't worry, Bill. We're still friends."

Old Joe did the same. Once when I came for a visit, Jim didn't run to greet me. I looked around for him. All I saw was Joe holding his index finger to his lips. When he saw he had caught my eye, he pointed to Jim. There was Jim snoring for all he was worth right next to the front stoop. I decided it wasn't a good time for a visit and passed by in silence. I nodded to Joe to let him know I understood.

Jim was the outgoing and friendly sort, even to politicians. Once when the lieutenant governor made a visit to Petoskey, the mayor was showing him around and they happened upon Joe and his dog. As usual, there stood Jim-ta-gu, his paw raised, waiting to "shake hands" with a new friend. The lieutenant governor obliged him.

An accompanying photographer called to them to look his way. The next day, the picture appeared in the *Northern Michigan Review*. There was the lieutenant governor with his best politician's smile showing as he shook hands with Jim-ta-gu. There was Jim-ta-gu giving the proper greeting he had been taught to do with his paw, looking at the camera, and clearly smiling.

Joe cut the picture out of the newspaper and showed it to everyone who would take time to look. When the picture was worn and in pieces, Joe would still put it together like a jigsaw puzzle. Then he would proudly step back so we could look at it.

Jim-ta-gu was a talented dog.

We once saw Joe slipping and sliding down an ice hill. Jim-ta-gu had the seat of Joe's pants in his teeth as he, too, slid along behind Joe on all fours. He held old Joe up on his feet!

As the years crept by, old Joe shuffled along slower and slower. Jim-ta-gu went slower too. He no longer ran circles around Joe. He just walked slowly at his side.

Then came the very sad time Joe got pneumonia and died. At Joe's wake, some Indians made the mistake of holding the old dog up to look at Joe in his casket. After the services, they put Joe's coffin in the hearse, and a long line of cars headed for the cemetery on the outskirts of town. Jim-ta-gu was too old to run alongside. He tried but kept falling. A car of young Indians stopped and put the dog in the backseat. The old dog whimpered when they lowered the casket into the ground.

After the burial, all the Indians asked what was to become of the old dog. A widow named Mrs. Miximony took him home with her. Every morning, Jim-ta-gu was to be seen walking up to the cemetery, where he stayed all day by Joe's grave. He stayed there until they chased him out at night.

Not surprisingly, the day came when the cemetery caretaker drove down to tell us Jim was lying dead on Joe's grave.

My brother and I ran up to the cemetery. Jim-ta-gu appeared to be sleeping. He was lying with his head on his paws, covered by a fine dusting of snow. The wind gently ruffled his hair. When Uncle Ike got there with a blanket, we carried Jim-ta-gu up to the woods overlooking the cemetery and buried him.

In my long life, I have seen only a few cases of what I can describe as "undying love." I like to think that old Joe and Jim-ta-gu represented just that. I like to think they are together again somewhere in another dimension where time is unending. I like to think such a great love as was between them deserves not to end. Not ever!

After Jim-ta-gu got his picture in the paper with the lieutenant governor, I started looking at talent with new eyes. It wasn't long before I started to see it all around me and in lots of different people.

Flop's talent was his skill in the woods. My sister, Muggs, was what we used to call "a looker." She was more than a beautiful Indian girl. Years later, I heard Marilyn Monroe talk about her "camera face." She said until she "put that on," she was just Norma Jean. As best I could tell, her camera face was something she locked into from the inside that turned her into Marilyn Monroe. Muggs never went into the movies, but after I heard Marilyn Monroe talk about her camera face, I knew Muggs had the very same talent.

We'd be walking down the street together, and no one would be giving us a second thought. Then Muggs would pop up with, "Bill, are you ready?"

I knew what she meant, and I would always groan. Within a few seconds we'd have people falling all over themselves trying to do things for her or be with her. I got in many a fight over Muggs's camera face.

People often told me I was born with golden vocal cords. And then there was Oakley. He was one of those lucky, multitalented guys. Music was one of his better talents. He couldn't read a note, but he was able to make the most beautiful music. He played what he called his "chromatic." I called it his "mouth organ," as did everyone else in Hungry Hollow. I'd learn much later in life that the proper name for the instrument was *harmonica*. It had a button on the side that, when pushed in, changed the half tones of the diatonic scale. Whenever I listen to the Harmonicats, I think of Oakley's music.

Most people think you just get up and sing with an orchestra. They think you sing when you want to and how you want to. They think the orchestra follows you. They are surprised to find out the orchestra members, also called "side men," don't know what the singer is doing. For example, the man on baritone sax can't pay attention to what the singer is doing because he's too busy playing and reading his own part. The *meter* is the only thing that makes everything come together as it should. The *meter* is the timing or as some call it, the rhythm. Everyone must stay within it. A singer or "side man" straying outside of it brings to life the most awful word in a musician's vocabulary—DISCORD!

Oakley and I always felt a person must be born with the instinct called "timing." We thought it was something that couldn't be taught. Of course, you can be shown what it is and how to use it. However, if it isn't a part of you, you might as well give up the idea of singing professionally. Without an instinct for timing, it doesn't matter how good your voice is. Oakley had a name for the instinct of timing. He called it the "in-the-groove feeling."

Before my voice changed as I entered adulthood, I had the high-pitched adolescent tones of a fourteen year old. Even so, I could sing.

One evening, after dinner, I was sitting on our front stoop when I saw Oakley walking towards our house. It's more accurate to say I heard Oakley before I saw him. He was playing his own rendition of "Sugar Blues" on his harmonica. He reached our front yard and stood there serenading me with the final few bars of the melody.

"Howdy, Cousin. What are you up to this fine evening?" he asked.

I clapped my appreciation of his song and said, "Just trying to stay cool."

"How about joining me in a song?"

"You name it. Start the intro, and I'll join in."

He played a few bars of "Pennies from Heaven," and I came in right on cue. We were having a great time doing all our favorites with slight variations in rhythm or key. My mother and father came outside to enjoy our spontaneous concert. To tell you the truth, we were concentrating so hard on what we were doing that we didn't even notice them. Soon several other neighbors had gathered to listen as well. When we finished "This Little Light of Mine," we were startled by the applause that followed. We spent the rest of that evening taking requests and performing them.

After that, our concerts became quite popular. We passed many good evenings entertaining ourselves and all of Hungry Hollow.

· 6 ·

Back to the Blanket

Scorched and dry from the heat wave, Petoskey was in trouble. Fire bells clanged night and day as fires devoured home after home. Undermanned and overworked, the city's fire department was on the verge of collapse. In Hungry Hollow, we knew that if fire struck our area, the red trucks would not arrive in time to save us. Our only defense was extra vigilance and plain old-fashioned luck. We knew our vigilance would last until the fall rains arrived. We hoped our luck would too.

It didn't. It ran out one sunny afternoon in August. The fire's cause remains a mystery to this day. Its devastation began before the smoke cleared. "Only one house burned" was carefully logged into the official record. A job well done and relief the fire was "contained" were the conclusions most come to after reading that report. Most, that is, except the family who called that one house home.

The Kewaygoshkums lived at the end of Sheridan in a very old and very dry house. Like every other house on the street, it had tar-paper roofing. Unlike other houses, it also had tar-paper siding. The combination of old, dry, and tar paper made the expression "firetrap" a perfect fit.

John Kewaygoshkum's panicked voice knocked the peace and calm right of Hungry Hollow that afternoon. It brought neighbors scurrying from every direction.

"Fire! Fire!" he kept yelling. Anna stood in the yard with their two youngest children clinging to her for all they were worth.

"Where's Lilly?" he shouted at her.

Before she could answer, he told the two little ones, "Stick with your mother."

The yelling and commotion had brought Leo Kewaygoshkum running home.

John told Anna, "I'll take Leo and find the rest. If any of them show up before we get back, keep them right here! OK?"

She nodded as tears were running down her cheek.

"Leo," John shouted at his son, "let's go find your brothers and sisters."

Without another word, they disappeared behind the house. Flames were now leaping in and around the front windows. Friends and neighbors who had rushed to the scene gathered in front of their house. For a few minutes no one moved or said a word.

The disaster unfolding before their eyes had them frozen in place. Tom Bush acted first. He ran to alert the fire department. When he returned, he started shouting orders.

"Don't just stand there gawking. Get anything you can find that'll hold water and meet me at the closest well."

We scattered. We dug through our belongings like madmen and rushed back. We were loaded down with buckets, pots, pans, and even bowls. Anything that could hold water had been carried to the well pump. The men took turns drawing the water as fast as they could. The rest of us lined up with containers in hand, ready to step into place as soon as the container held by the person in front of us was full. Timing was everything. No one wanted to waste one drop of the precious water. Another line going all the way to the fire had formed. As each container was filled, it was passed towards the fire. When it reached the last person, he or she would toss the water on the flames and then race back to the end of the line to start all over again. All of this effort didn't help, as the fire won hands down. I felt we'd have done just as well to stand there and spit.

The sound of a roaring fire is unique. On a cold winter night its music warms your soul. The cracking and snapping it made that afternoon hammered defeat into each and every one of us. The line got smaller and smaller as the fire raged on and our stamina wore out. With nothing else we could do, we stood arm in arm and watched the fire consume everything John, Anna, and their nine children called home.

A fire truck did eventually show up, but it was too late. The house and everything in it was gone.

Tom Bush was so upset he started talking to whoever would listen.

"Those fire guys weren't in too much of a hurry to get here. No, they had that important grass fire on the other side of town to put out first. I knew it'd be this way. Folks like them are never in a hurry when it comes to helping folks like us."

He went on and on in a voice loud enough for everyone, including the firemen, to hear. His wife slipped her arm around his and whispered something. He jerked away and walked off by himself. Several minutes later, he came back and tapped her on her shoulder. Arm in arm, they walked home in silence.

Our family stood by the Kewaygoshkums from the beginning of the fire, lending our support and comfort. My mother and Anna had been best friends for a long time. Now, the only thing she could do for her friend was put her arm around her. John told my dad he was sure the fire had started outside the house.

As the fire dwindled, friends and neighbors focused on finding the Kewaygoshkums a place to spend the night. No one had enough room to take in the whole family, so they were parceled out to several homes.

The next day, people gathered in front of what had been the Kewaygoshkum home. The women helped Anna poke around the ashes just in case something had escaped the fire. Nothing had. Anna began to cry and decided she'd had enough. All the women walked to our house to share hot coffee. Everyone wanted some comfort.

John and my father stood side by side watching the whole process. They didn't talk, and they remained there even when the women left. They just kept looking at the ashes and smoldering coals.

My dad was the first to speak. "Got any idea what you are going to do?"

"Anna and I were up most of the night. I don't believe I saw a single star. Something about that seemed fitting, given what we're facing."

My dad agreed.

"We don't have anywhere to go or the money to get us there if we did. The more we talked and tried to figure what to do, the more darkness seemed to close in on us. It wasn't 'til after dawn that it occurred to me. I told Anna there's only one thing to do. We gotta go back to the blanket."

My father looked at John and raised one eyebrow. His practical Scotch nature made him question John's solution.

John picked up on that right away and said, "I know it's been before our time when people lived off the land. I figure we'll make our way just like they did. There are all kinds of berries and other fruit that can be had just for the picking. Wild onions, dandelion greens, and milkweed are plentiful. When you stop to think about it, there are lots of good things to eat for the taking, things the Great Spirit meant us to have. We'll fish in Bear River and Little Traverse. We'll hunt, and I'll snare rabbits. When I was a boy, my mother used to store things like potatoes, carrots, and apples right in the ground. Anna knows how to dry fruits and vegetables. We'll make it. You wait and see!"

Later that day, John and Anna went for a walk in the woods to find their new home. Near the bay, they came upon a stand of poplars sheltering a small clearing. A small breeze off the bay was filling the woods with the special music only poplars can make when strummed. The fresh scent of the bay told them their water needs could be easily met there. They didn't need to talk things over. They hurried back to the hollow to get their kids and show them their new home.

True to his word of following the old ways, John cut lodge poles and began to dig the holes for them. Anna and the kids went off to gather the birch bark to cover their lodge. Digging was hard work. He had stopped to catch his breath when he noticed a horse and wagon coming up the dirt road.

"Hey John!" a voice called to him. "How's it going?"

A big grin spread across John's face. An old army buddy, Pete Polson, was the wagon driver. John put down his shovel and walked to greet him. He and Pete had been through a lot together. They'd faced hunger, cold, and even death in the trenches of World War I.

"Pete, what the heck brings you down here?"

"Aw, not much really. I heard about the fire. It broke my heart. How are you doing?"

"We're making it."

"I can see that. Doesn't surprise me one bit. I heard about your plans. Great idea! Just great! I was trying to think of how I could help when I remembered something I had stored away. I took the liberty of bringing it down here for you. Now don't feel like you got to take it or anything. I can see you're getting along in a good way."

He walked to the back of the wagon and pulled back a tarp. Inside the wagon was a surplus army tent.

John could hardly speak, he was so touched by his friend's offer of help.

"That ought to fit quite nicely" was all he could get out.

They unloaded the tent and made quick work of putting it up.

When they finished, John let out a whoop and shouted, "Praise God! Now let it rain!"

Pete left soon after that. He'd taken time out of a busy schedule to help an old friend, and now it was time to get back to work. John watched him drive away. Back on the main road, Pete turned to get a final look at the tent. It stood firmly anchored in the woods. He spotted John and waved.

As John returned the wave, he felt the muscles in his neck and shoulders relax. It was a good feeling to know his family would have plenty of sleeping room and would be high and dry.

Anna and the kids soon returned loaded down with birch. They could hardly believe what they saw.

"Pete Polson!" Anna exclaimed. "I can't remember the last time we saw him."

"I know. He heard about our troubles and stopped everything to help us out. Friends like Pete don't come around the corner every day."

Those words were hardly out of John's mouth when a long line of friends started down the dirt lane to the Kewaygoshkums' new home. They were a sight to behold! This one carried a blanket, that one brought a kettle, and still another brought an old chair. My mother brought a cast-iron skillet and a few forks and spoons. My dad brought a double-bit ax, a handsaw, and a sharpening file. The steady stream of Indians continued into the evening. They had very little to spare. It was their deep caring for John, Anna, and their children that turned their sacrifices that day into the joy of sharing.

The Kewaygoshkums were not alone in the woods on the beach. A few Indian men had built little shanties out of driftwood and other materials they could find. Normally, they kept to themselves. That changed when the Kewaygoshkums moved in. One of the men, Mob Lawrence, brought John a supply of fishing line and hooks. He also showed John the best places to fish on the big rocks.

The spirit of sharing born on that day soon spread. Ben Thompson, a white farmer, came and told John and Anna to bring their children and glean all they could use from his harvest fields. He also let them have fruit from his orchards. In his church basement, Reverend Weaver had clothing that had been gathered from his flock. He called on the Kewaygoshkums and invited John and Anna to come and help themselves to whatever they could use.

John and Anna walked the streets every day looking for any kind of work. John was willing to do anything he could do, including mowing lawns or washing windows. Anna offered to do housework of any kind. They would often take food in the place of money. Every little bit helped.

John told my dad about his bartering work for food and joked, "You can't eat money."

A deputy sheriff came to camp one day. One look told John and Anna he brought trouble.

"You folks are squatting here, and that's against the law. This property belongs to the state," he told them.

John thought awhile before he answered, "You'll just have to put us all in jail, Deputy, 'cause we don't have any other place to be."

The deputy didn't say another word. He left and never came back.

The visit did cause John a few sleepless nights. He thought about moving and feared maybe his children would be taken from him. He came to the conclusion that that would be more than he could bear. After all the wonderful help they'd received, the deputy's attitude was hard for him to understand. He decided to talk over his concerns with my dad.

"You'd think they would try to help someone in great need. No, they try to hurt us even more. They wish us Indians would just disappear! We're not the ones who intruded on them. It's the other way around. Even when we try to stay off by ourselves, they won't leave us alone."

There was very little my dad could say to a man living on the edge of survival. He was far from alone. Everyone in Hungry Hollow lived within sight of that edge. President Roosevelt kept telling us that the only thing we had to fear was fear itself. That night, as we walked back home, I thought about the president's words. I wanted to believe what he said was true. I wanted to believe we could outlast the Depression. I just didn't know how.

· 7 ·

The Iron Monster

As September rolled in, the heat wave rolled out. Frank's back porch was once again fit for gathering on. The community took advantage of the very first day temperatures were back in the seventies.

Isaac Naska and Paul Day-Bird sat in their usual places. Frank Michigan had moved one chair to the left of Isaac. Today, they wouldn't be telling stories. They would be listening to them.

My mother's uncle had agreed to sit in the honored *Ah-soo-can-nah-nah,* or storyteller's chair.

"It was in the moon of the ripe berries," he began. "The summer had been good to the berries by giving them lots of water to drink and plenty of sunshine and warm air to grow in. Mmmmmmm. I can still see those big plump beauties just asking to be picked and eaten."

He rubbed his belly and winked at us as he asked, "Are you with me, nephews? Can you see those berries?"

"Yes!" we shouted in unison.

And we could. Our mouths were even watering.

"That's good," he replied. "One morning, about the time the sun was getting up, I heard a knock on my door. I couldn't figure who could be at my door at that hour. There was only one way to find out."

A broad smile spread across his face. We laughed and elbowed one another.

"Who was it?" we wanted to know.

"'Good morning, Grandson,' a familiar voice greeted me. 'Are you feeling a little lazy today?'

"'No, I'm surprised we didn't pass each other on my way in,' I teased.

"'I thought as much,' my grandmother said, wagging her finger at me in jest. 'Have you heard how good the berries are this year?'

"'I'd heard something like that. I don't suppose this early visit has anything to do with berries,' I teased.

"She laughed and nodded her head.

"'When I looked out the window this morning, I couldn't help but think it was a perfect day for berry picking,' I said.

"'I was thinking the very same thing,' she replied.

"Her laughter always warmed my heart. Berry picking it would be. As we headed out the door, she picked up the basket she had brought to hold the berries.

"'Grandson, don't forget our lunch.'

"A second basket filled with goodies and covered with a small white cloth sat near my front stoop. I picked it up but didn't look inside. I wanted to wait 'til lunchtime to see what goodies she had prepared. We reached the mouth of the Bear River, where I had my canoe beached. She held my arm as she stepped into the canoe. After she had centered herself, I handed her the baskets. Then, with a good send-off push, I jumped into the front seat. We were off!

"With Be-dos-ga behind us, or Petoskey if you want to use the English name, our attention turned to the beauty surrounding us. The water was like glass. My paddle cut through it so smoothly I created very little wake. When we reached the shore of Little Traverse Bay, then known as Kegomic (meaning 'the place of the fish'), we beached our canoe at Menonaquay (whose name meant 'woman's place'). We had to walk inland about three miles before we reached Grandmother's favorite spot. She'd been bringing me there as far back as I could remember. Her grandmother had shown it to her years before. It had lots of bushes filled with plump, ripe blueberries, and it also held many good memories for our family.

"I placed our lunch basket in a small clearing. We went to work picking and eating. The berries were so ripe and sweet you didn't even have to chew them. They just melted in your mouth."

He smiled and rubbed his belly again. Giggles and laughter spread through the room.

"For the next couple of hours we did a lot of picking, eating, and walking. I decided it was time to stretch my back. I took my time about it. Just when I was ready to get back to work, I noticed a wide path had been cut through the woods. *Who would do such a thing? I wondered.*

"I called Grandmother over to where I was standing. We walked closer to get a better look. In the middle of that path lay two strips of iron. Cozied up side by side, they weren't making a sound.

"'Why would anyone tear apart the earth to lay down two sticks?' Grandmother asked.

"'I've never seen such a thing,' I told her.

"We knelt down next to them. They looked cold and silent, but when I touched one of them, I got the surprise of my life. It was alive! It growled and shook my hand! I jumped back. My heart was thumping so fast I thought it might burst right through my chest!"

"'Let's get . . .' were the only words I heard my grandmother say.

"A scream, louder than anything we'd ever heard, filled the air. I grabbed my ears in pain. I would have sworn a sharp knife was twisting into each of them. What unknown beast was stalking us?

"I forced open my eyes only to see a huge black monster with one big eye in the middle of its head roaring straight at us!

"'WE'RE DOOMED!' I screamed at the top of my lungs. 'IT'S ATTACKING! RUUUUUUNNN FOR YOUR LIFE!'

"The power and size of that beast running through the woods shook the earth itself. Its elbows pumped furiously up and down, giving it more speed than anything I'd ever seen. It bore down on us, never wavering one inch off its path. Racing towards us as it was, I knew it could only have one purpose in its mind—dinner!

"I grabbed Grandmother's hand and tried to drag her to safety with me. It was too late. She fell to the ground in a heap. Before I could gather my wits about me, my feet were running to the canoe.

"I tell you, nephews," he said wiping his forehead, "I've never run so fast as I did that day. I even found myself passing Waboose! He was so surprised, he stopped dead in his tracks just to watch me!"

We all giggled at what a sight that must have been. A rabbit stopping to watch my grand uncle run!

"When I finally caught up with myself, the roar was gone. Only the birds and crickets remained. Had that horrible thing really left? Could it still get me? I knew I had to go back and find my grandmother. My legs were shaking so badly, I wasn't sure they were going to be able to carry me. I felt all numb and sick on the inside. What would I do if I found that the iron monster had taken her? The rustling sounds had stopped. I held my breath, hoping I couldn't be seen.

"My grandmother stepped into the clearing! She'd escaped the iron monster! Her hair was going every which way, and her dress was torn in a few places. All that mattered, though, was she wasn't hurt. She'd fainted dead away. Neither of us knew why the monster had passed her by. We were just thankful it had. We hugged each other for all we were worth and then sat down to recover. As soon as we had our strength again, we made our way back to the canoe and hurried home.

"Once we got there, no one would believe us. I was glad my grandmother had seen the great iron monster. She was a respected elder. Ordinarily, her words went unchallenged. However, the story of the iron monster brought a torrent of questions. She wasn't bothered. No one could change the facts. It was as simple as that. The sun slipped beneath the horizon with the discussion still going strong.

"At dawn, a pack of well-armed men headed to the waterfront. They were determined to see the iron one with their own eyes. I watched them disappear among the waves. I wondered if the beast would reveal himself to so many strong men.

"Morning passed without news. Early afternoon came and went. Just before dark, shouts could be heard coming from the shore. The men had returned! All of them! Everyone rushed to greet the incoming canoes. No one spoke until the last canoe had been safely beached. It was true! What we'd seen was true. Who knew what to make of this beast? It was too strong and too swift for our men to hunt. The best news was that it didn't even notice our men. They were able to return without a battle. Much time would pass before we learned more about the great beast. Sadly, the berry-picking place, with all of its wonderful memories, was lost to my family the day the iron monster came roaring through our world.

"The iron monster turned out to be something the white men used to carry them places. They called it a steam engine. The monster screaming at the top of its lungs was really an engine blowing its whistle to warn us from its path. This proved to be the first of many things that would change our lives forever. So, nephews, be careful of this thing called 'progress.' It may decide to stalk you when you least expect it!"

· 8 ·

Run to Freedom

Flop, Oakley, and I were proud our uncle was such a good storyteller. He was still receiving congratulations for his story when an Indian named John Mik-sa-be came into Frank's for a haircut. He and his wife, Delia, lived in nearby Bay Shore. When the heat wave broke, Delia had decided accompanying her husband to Frank's would be a good opportunity to catch up on visiting. Everyone was glad to see them. As is always the case when Indians gather, there was lots of laughing and joking to be done. It was difficult to decide what Frank enjoyed the most—his work or all the good times the gatherings on his back porch provided. During all the commotion, he never stopped combing and clipping. After awhile, things quieted down and John decided to share a story of a good deed the Indians had done for people of other races.

"In those days, when the seasons changed hands the people gathered around the long-house fire to discuss the fate of the community. There was never any arguing or ill will involved in these gatherings, because each person who wanted one had a turn to speak. Of course, some opinions were more highly regarded than others were, but this could always change according to the topic being discussed. My grandfather was known for his wisdom and fairness. He'd seen many changes in his time and had weathered many sorrows and losses. If I close my eyes, I can still see him in the light of those fires, sharing what was on his mind. His words never failed to cut through the night chill like a warm blade.

"He would say, 'As long as you have the strength to look for the sun, you'll never be broken. It is good to get in this habit, because when darkness sets in, you'll know your hope lies in finding where the sun is shining. Remember, it always is; we're the ones who lose sight of it.'

"Discussions about the dark times took up many fires," John said. "However, the elders always warned us not to feel special. They reminded us darkness had always fallen upon our people from time to time. They stressed that the important part of listening to the stories about darkness was learning how to find our way through it.

"When I think about stories of coming through darkness, one comes to mind that had its beginning at one of those long-house gatherings.

"My father was just a boy. For some time there'd been talk in the long house of people in the South being bought and sold and made to work against their will for the profit of others. No one agreed with this kind of treatment towards others. There were many who voiced concern that that fate might also lie in our future.

"'We still have our freedom,' my grandfather said when he received the talking stick. 'Today, that is our sunshine. I would caution us against being too content in this light. I would ask we not forget there are those searching for it as we speak.'

"He was referring to the fact that some of the enslaved African people were able to run away," John explained. "Their goal was to get to Canada, where slavery was not allowed. In those times, the seven routes that were used were of common knowledge among our people. All but one of them ended near Detroit. If the freedom seekers could travel as far north as that, the Detroit River was all that stood between them and freedom. Our people often helped them on that final leg. It was fairly easy at that point, because the river was lined on both sides by woods. The seventh route ran due north out of Chicago. It was a different story. It jigged and jagged back and forth through the woods, always hugging the shore of Lake Michigan as much as possible. The part of that route that ran through Emmet County was called the Freedom Road. It was run in most part by the people known as the Quakers.

"Many times, the Quakers called upon the Indians for help. This was especially true when slave hunters closely pursued them.

No one is as good at hiding something or someone in the woods as Indians are. It was only natural for the Quakers and others to look to us for this kind of help.

"Sometimes the slave hunters bottled up the other six routes to freedom and only the seventh could be used. That particular night, a request for help had been made by an Indian called 'Black Skin,' who ran an underground railway near Grand Rapids. He was tall and quite handsome. In cold weather, he always wore a beautiful black coat made of black squirrel skins. His striking appearance in this coat quickly earned him his name.

"My grandfather's speech ended by saying, 'I, for one, feel we should honor this request. There is no time to waste.'

"After he finished, it was decided. Our people would do everything they could to help. As it turned out, our help would come just in the nick of time. The other six routes had been stopped up by the slave catchers for weeks. No one could predict when they would be safe enough to travel again. Black Skin's small depot was crowded to the point of overflowing. Normally, he'd escort his visitors north himself. This time he knew he'd need help to avoid the hunters who would soon be breathing down his neck. He sent word north for help and waited. My grandfather was one of the Indians who answered that call.

"Now, you may be wondering why there were slave catchers in Michigan. After all, we were in a state where one man being a slave to another was outlawed. The answer is a simple one, but it is not very pretty. Some men in our state government had made a law allowing slave hunters to operate in our state. It has been said that they were dishonest and were paid a large sum of money by wealthy slave owners to make this law. I myself do not know this to be true, because I never met these men and I never saw any money exchanged. All this happened long before I was born. I only offer this to you because it was the explanation given to me for such a bad law.

"My grandfather was not the only one to volunteer that night. Ten Indians from northern Michigan set out through the woods towards Black Skin's depot. Their trip south was uneventful but swift.

"In the outer perimeter of the camp, they came upon an Indian called 'Coo.' 'Coo' was short for 'Coo Coo,' or, roughly translated, 'Owl Man.' He was on guard duty and was very happy to see his northern cousins. He gave them directions to the hidden camp and said they were expected. Just outside of the depot, Black Skin came out to greet his northern cousins. He thanked them for their quick response and told them the ex-slaves were rested, well fed, and ready to travel. He also told them he was very glad some of the runaways would be taken off his hands.

"Once in camp, Black Skin invited his northern cousins to share a fire and have something hot to eat. He warned them that the dogs the slave catchers were using had strong noses and could track through almost anything. The dogs had never been seen in that part of the country before. My father passed this story along to me, and he told me that after listening to the description his father gave, he figured these dogs were bloodhounds.

"In any case, the tracking abilities of the dogs worried Black Skin. He wanted the Indians from the north to know what they were facing. Everyone listened with great interest. One of the Indians from Burt Lake spoke up. He said he couldn't make any promises in as much as he'd never encountered these dogs, but he did have some medicine with him he thought might be helpful. He claimed no dog he knew anything about would follow a trail where this dust had been sprinkled. He said he was willing to bet these new trackers wouldn't either. He sat back down and waited.

"Some of the men scoffed at this 'medicine.' This was in their right to do so, as they would be putting their lives on the line. Mik-sa-be didn't opine one way or the other. He just said he knew the man from Burt Lake used the powder before and hadn't been followed by any dogs when he did.

"Discussion around the fire continued while some of the Indians from the north decided they should teach the runaways how to *woptahn*. They would be using this special kind of step, or gait, on their trip north. For as long as any of them could remember, woodland Indians had used it when traveling over land. Some called it the 'dog trot.' The gait was a shuffling-type step in which one foot was always on the ground. Woptahn was faster than walking and slower than running. Using that gait, a person could travel for miles without tiring. Much to the relief of the Indians, the runaways had no trouble picking up the step.

"Black Skin's northern cousins had come prepared to usher their new friends to freedom. They had packed provisions of smoked fish and water for the journey north. As dawn approached, it became clear nothing could be resolved regarding the effectiveness of the powder against the tracking ability of the dogs. Any trip north would be a risk to everyone taking it. There was agreement to try the powder and keep as vigilant as possible.

"Without waiting for dawn, the ten Indians headed north, guiding twenty ex-slaves. In their charge were mostly men, a few women, and no children. They went by twos, led by an Indian, with an Indian in the rear and one Indian on each side. The rest of the Indians flanked the entire group but remained out of sight.

"Summer and fall had been dry up north. Everything was as brown and dry as it is now. It was late enough in the year that the leaves were already on the ground. As this small group started their run to the Straits of Mackinac, the newcomers made quite a racket as they crunched the dry leaves underfoot. My grandfather said the Indians were understanding of these freedom seekers, as they were new to the woods. He also said he soon was as worried about the slave hunters hearing them as he was about their dogs smelling them. The Great Spirit must have been watching over them, because mile after mile they went undetected. When they got close to Little Traverse Bay, or, as we called it then, Kegomic (meaning 'the place of the fish'), it started to rain. It was really just a drizzle, but it was enough to make the forest floor wet.

"The damp ground made them able to travel as silent as ghosts. The group was rounding the east end of Kegomic when they hit their first bit of trouble. The flanking Indians startled the ex-slaves when they showed themselves. Without a word being said, they motioned for the group to hunker down and be silent. White men had been spotted just to the west.

"Two Indians set out to follow the white men. After a few miles, they 'accidentally' allowed their paths to cross. It turned out these men were working for the Grand Rapids and Indiana Railroad and were studying good routes to the northland. They weren't the dreaded slave hunters!

"The Indians who had remained with the group decided it was too dangerous to wait for a report. They put their emergency plan into action. Using hand signals and no words, each Indian took two or three black people and headed in a direction away from where they had just gathered. These smaller groups made their way as fast as possible to a preset rendezvous near the Straits of Mackinac. The two Indian scouts discovered the emergency plan had been enacted, and they hurried on to the designated meeting place. The rendezvous was a joyous one, and the group continued their journey.

"On the south shore of the straits, the Chippewas were waiting. Their job was the hardest. They had to get the black people across the open waters of the straits. The shortest distance across was about five miles. They would be in plain sight the whole way. They planned to make their crossing under the cover of night, but they knew a practiced eye could still make them out. They were counting on the slave hunters to have neither the eyes nor the skills to keep up with them in the cold, treacherous waters of the straits.

"The wind was whipping and blowing with a fierceness that was usual at that time of year. The ex-slaves were clearly frightened of the crossing. Who could blame them? The water stretched out as far as the eye could see. The travelers would only have a canoe between them and a cold death. The prospect of freedom proved to be a stronger motivation than their fear of death. They climbed into the three 'war canoes' that were waiting on the beach. Each canoe was capable of holding eight people. The canoes were silent and fast. In the right hands, they were also very safe. Of course, these newcomers had no way of knowing that. My grandfather had to admire their courage. They were willing to put their lives in the hands of total strangers just for a taste of real freedom. He said he was proud to have kept company with such praiseworthy individuals.

"The Ottawas bid the ex-slaves and the Chippewas good-bye, and they wished them well as they shoved off in their canoes, bound for the opposite shore of the Straits of Mackinac. They watched until the dim outline of the far shore and the night swallowed them up. Then they began their walk, slowly, toward their home area.

"Sometime later, a Chippewa traveler named John Misscocamon, whose grandfather was one of the Indians who accompanied the ex-slaves after the Chippewas took over from the Ottawas at the Straits of Mackinac, told this account of the finish of that particular episode.

" 'Well rested from their wait for the Ottawas and spurred on by the anxiousness of the ex-slaves to reach Canada, the Chippewas sprinted across the Straits of Mackinac without incidence. The next day, they rested near what is now called St. Ignace. As night set in, they guided their charges through the forest to the St. Marys River where they made their way to the narrowest point between Neebish Island and Potaganning Bay.

" 'Back in the canoes they went. Every few minutes, a Chippewa in the lead canoe would up and study the stars. From this he could tell the time of the night and gauge their progress. A few moments later, they crossed the boundary into Canada and were greatly elated and relieved.'

"My grandfather only made this one trip with the former slaves. He didn't know for sure how many other times the Indians helped out. He knew there were some, but he always said the number of missions didn't matter. What mattered was that the Indian people detested the practice of slavery and did what they could to help end it."

· 9 ·

Black and Brown

Fall rains quenched the last signs of Petoskey's heat wave. This good news did not offset the continuing bad news of the Depression. Every city and town in the country was filled with people struggling to survive. In Hungry Hollow, our diet had been reduced to three kinds of meal—cornmeal, oatmeal, and miss-a-meal. Figuring out how to get the first two took a lot of inventiveness.

The best example of what I'm talking about was an Indian named Sam Prickett. One day after school, I happened to see him at work. He was one of the lucky ones who happened to get a few hours of work that week. I stopped to watch him. A very rough, thick rope was sliding through his gloved hands. Sweat glistened on his forehead. His muscles strained as he labored. After a few minutes, he stopped and took off his work gloves. I thought he was going to take a break, but I was wrong. He carefully tucked the gloves into the top of his pants and took up the rope again. It slid through his bare hands!

What could he be thinking? That rope will skin his hands for sure!

I couldn't stand my curiosity one more second, so I shouted, "What are you doing? That rope will tear your hands to shreds."

Without stopping his work or even looking in my direction, he hollered back, "Goosah," which means "son," "I can get new skin. I can't get new gloves!"

Worry was about the only thing not in short supply. You could see it wearing lines into faces. You could hear it in the hushed tones of day-to-day conversations. Everyone said worry was a dead-end street. They claimed it did nothing good for you. Still, everyone did it. They couldn't help themselves. My parents were no exception. I could feel the tension in my mother's hugs as she sent us off to bed. Lines began to cover her face like a blanket. I went to sleep to the sound of my father's sighs as he rocked by the fire each night.

We kids didn't fare any better. I often wished I could ease my parents' hardships by securing a job. My desires were pipe dreams. The long line of men trying and failing to get work always brought that home to me. I wanted to do something—anything. There was nothing I could do. When school started again that year, I was relieved. It gave my mind someplace to let go of my troubles.

I was usually up and on my way long before Flop or Muggs. B.B. was the other early riser in our neighborhood. Each morning, he would always be waiting for me when I started down Sheridan Street. I'd run to catch up to him, and we'd go on to school. We got to be good friends—the kind that could share anything.

Everyone said B.B. had a good head on his shoulders. He sure didn't mind using it. Never was that more true than the day he earned his nickname, "B.B."

B.B. had an uncommon hunger for an education. His grand-father was the first to spot it in him. Every chance he got, he would remind B.B. that education was everything. He told him it was the key to all the wants and needs he'd have in life. "Schoolhousing" was what he called it.

B.B. took to his grandfather's encouragement like Flop had taken to our dad's hunting abilities. He poured his heart into his schoolhousing.

That morning, B.B. was waiting for me on Sheridan Street as usual. He was whistling and rocking back and forth on his heels. I waved and picked up my pace. As I got closer, I stopped in my tracks. My eyes grew as big as saucers. He had on one BLACK shoe and one BROWN shoe!

Being good chums like we were, I didn't want to say anything. In the few steps it took me to catch up with him, I realized it was too late. My face had already been shouting at him. I didn't know what to do. I felt just plain awful for him and for me.

"How's it going?"

B.B. studied me for a few seconds. His face did some talking too. Embarrassment cuts deep.

"I was hoping it wouldn't show. Yesterday, when I was doing my chores, my left shoe gave up on me. I asked Ma if she could fix it. She tried her best. I have to give her that. Then, without saying a word, she got up, went straight to the trash, and threw it in. There wasn't a thing that could be done to fix it."

I knew this was true, because he'd been tripping over that shoe for weeks. My shoes weren't much better, but at least they were still on my feet. We walked along in silence for awhile, then I remembered his father had just gotten a job.

"Did something happen to your father's new job? I hope all the celebrating didn't jinx it or something."

"No, he still has the job."

"Couldn't he use a little bit of his paycheck to buy you some shoes?"

"That's the first thing I thought," B.B. said.

"I talked to him about it. I told him straight out what'd happened."

"And?"

"He heard me out. Then he asked to see the shoe. I ran and got it out of the trash and handed it to him."

"Then what?"

"He looked at it for the longest time. After turning it every which way, he let out a big sigh."

"'No doubt about it. This shoe is a goner. Looks like a new pair is the only way to go,' he told me.

"My heart just about leapt out of my chest for joy, but my father stopped it cold.

"'Hold on a minute,' he said. 'Before you get too happy, you need to know I don't get paid 'til next month. I don't see any way to get your shoes before then. You can't go to school without 'em. You'll have to stay home. I know a month sounds like a long time, but that's the best I can do. I promise you your shoes will be the first thing I buy when I get paid.'

"I've never seen my dad look like that. I would have done anything to make him feel better. I told him not to worry. I could always catch up."

Then he added, with a smile coming across his face, "I even volunteered you to bring me makeup lessons."

I nodded to let him know he could count on me.

"After that things got even more quiet. My dad went outside to cut some wood, and my mom made herself busy with supper. I just sat there looking at my foot. Then it hit me. I put two socks on my shoeless foot and took off for the dump. I thought for sure I could find another shoe. I scoured every inch of that dump. I was there 'til way after dark."

B.B. then pointed at his left foot. "This was the best I could do. Too big and black to boot. I almost threw it back, but when I got ready to pitch it, I just couldn't do it. Facts are facts. The sooner you face them the better. And the fact of this matter was that this old shoe was the best I was going to do until my dad's first paycheck. When I got home, I stuffed one of my socks in the toe. That fixed one problem. Sort of. I figure it'll work all right for a month."

He stopped walking and grabbed my arm. "I just didn't want to miss all that school."

I knew what would happen when we got to school. I had to warn him.

"You must be crazy to go to school with those shoes. Those white kids are going to hound you!"

I was wasting my breath. It was plain to see his ears were turned off. I shrugged my shoulders and we went on. The sounds of our school chums waiting for the doors to open filled our ears. As always, they were hanging out in groups. It didn't take long for the group we feared most to spot B.B.'s shoes. They wasted no time getting down to the business of having their fun. They pointed at his feet and guffawed. They slapped their thighs and roared with laughter! They called him names. At first, B.B. tried to ignore them. However, they weren't about to stop hounding him, and hound him they did!

I wanted to crawl into a hole and take my friend with me. Not

B.B. When he realized they weren't going to be ignored, he turned and stood his ground. That got their attention. They glared. We glared. I got ready to fight.

There's no turning back now.

Then B.B. did something I will never forget. A big smile crossed his face, and he broke into a laugh! They narrowed their eyes, unsure of how to take him. He pointed at his shoes and laughed even louder. That did it. They went back to laughing and pointing. B.B. roared the loudest of all! He kept laughing 'til his eyes filled with tears.

Saved by the bell! The school bell, that is. The other kids took off in a race to be first to enter the building. We took our time.

I'll never forget the sight of B.B. walking up those school steps in one brown shoe and one black shoe. After that day, we nicknamed him "B.B.," which was short for "Black and Brown."

As you might guess, B.B. got his education. He earned straight A's. That day made me think B.B. was headed for good things. I was right. He kept his passion for learning. He walked out of Hungry Hollow into one success after another. He went to college on the G.I. Bill, a right he earned in World War II. B.B. settled in Austin, Texas, where he became a Texas Ranger. He's not known as B.B. anymore. He's earned a different name. "Captain Carrier" is how he's known now. You won't find his fellow Rangers calling him anything less.

As important as regular schooling was to B.B., he would be the first to admit that schools aren't always made of brick and mortar and that teachers don't always hold degrees from universities. Like the rest of us, he liked attending Mrs. Greenleaf's school. She convened classes in her backyard. She was content to leave the subjects of reading, writing, and arithmetic to the public schools. Her curriculum included wisdom, compassion, and love of the earth and each other. I believe her teaching credentials came straight from the Creator Himself.

She didn't believe in preaching. No one ever accused her of holding church or trying to be a preacher. She probably would have told you she was a just storyteller. If you were looking to be entertained by what she did, you would have gotten that for sure and then some. I think the best thing about her stories were the meanings they planted. You could never tell when one of those seeds would take root and sprout into your life. Perhaps you would meet a situation that called for you to have a little more humility. As if by magic, a big buck she'd once told us about would suddenly come bounding through your mind. You'd remember what had happened when he misplaced his pride and that was usually enough to steer your life path in a better direction. If you were feeling like you were on the bottom of the heap of humanity, memories of those little gatherings would likely flood in and help wash away your self-doubt. Most every Indian child I ever knew hurried as fast as they could go to get to those gatherings. Kids who misbehaved at regular schools or even refused to study sat cross-legged, and gave Mrs. Greenleaf their total attention. At Mrs. Greenleaf's, they knew they were among their very own kind. At this "school" they were not harassed because of their ragged (but clean) clothing. They were not looked down upon because of their tan skin. They were loved. They didn't have to achieve or perform to get this love either. It was handed out just because they needed it.

I don't know of any rocket scientists or brain surgeons who came from that group. There was no way to teach them there what they needed to know to become those things. However, many a faithful, hardworking husband and father came from those gatherings. There were also wives and mothers whose ethics and standards were formed in these groups. Future tribal leaders often got their origins in Mrs. Greenleaf's learning circles.

The first time I can remember attending one, I was with Oakley. We were too old to sit with the little kids gathered around her and too young to know why we wanted to be a part of her circle.

"There they are again," Oakley told me one day, pointing to Mrs. Greenleaf. "Is it just me, or are there more and more kids in that group?"

I couldn't really give him an answer. I'd been so interested in following Oakley around, I hadn't paid much attention to the little kids' sessions.

"Never mind," Oakley said, taking me off the hook. "Let's listen in for a few minutes."

"It was the kind of cold that makes squeaky noises under your feet when you walk," Mrs. Greenleaf was saying.

"In fact, it was so cold, it was dangerous to be anywhere near a tree," she told them.

This definitely got their attention and ours.

"How come?" they all wanted to know.

I was glad they asked her this, because I was wondering the very same thing myself.

"Well," she explained. "Trees have a liquid cell sap that runs in their veins just like you and I have blood running in ours. The cold temperatures made the sap in the trees freeze, causing their insides to swell and even explode. The young elms were mostly likely to do this.

"In the middle of all these goings on, a little bird sat. He had skinny little legs and tiny feet. He knew they were in danger of freezing as solid as the sap in the surrounding trees. To make things worse, Mi-jeab-wis, the evil west wind, began to blow. He could feel Mi-jeab-wis draining the last of his strength away. He also knew death would soon pay him a visit if he didn't do something for himself.

"He gathered the last bit of his reserve and flew down to Cedar Swamp. In the middle of the swamp, he found an old, thick cedar tree. He wriggled into the very middle of the thick branches and locked his feet onto a limb. He puffed up his feathers until he looked like a ball, and then he lowered himself down until his scraggly legs were covered. A very welcome feeling of warmth spread all over him. For the first time in a very long time, he had hope. He settled down to see what the weather would do.

"Mi-jeab-wis did its best to penetrate those thick cedar branches. Try as it might, it could only rock the tree back and forth.

The gentle rocking brought a deep peace to the little bird. He put his head under one wing and fell asleep. He didn't stir again until the next morning. His little head popped from beneath his wing. He listened. To his delight, he heard only silence. He flew out of his shelter into the bright, warm sun. It was glittering like a million diamonds on the new snow. The little bird flew over to last summer's dried sunflower stalks and feasted on the delicious seeds he found there.

"Now children, what lesson did the little bird teach us today?"

I felt Oakley's hands cover both my ears. He gently nudged me away from where we'd been standing.

Out of earshot he asked, "So what do you think Mrs. Greenleaf's story was trying to tell us?"

"The bird took action. He did something about his problem. He didn't just stand around and complain."

Oakley burst out laughing and said, "By golly, you might make it yet, Bill! You're not half as dumb as I thought you were!"

I knew that was Oakley's way of kidding me, especially when I'd done something that pleased him.

"We'd best get to it," he said.

We had a lawn to mow and 15 cents to earn for our efforts.

· 10 ·

Three Potatoes Equals
One Movie

The Sheridan Street Rats were restless. The opening of deer season meant trigger-happy hunters flocked to the woods. They shot anything or anyone that moved. No questions asked.

For a grand total of 30 minutes out of the last 30 days, the sun had fought its way through the blanket of gray covering Petoskey. The sharp fall winds off the bay, armed with freezing rain, had put an end to our touch football games. Driving us off the football field wasn't enough for this formidable opponent. The little warmth it contained kept lakes and ponds from freezing into ice rinks and kept hills from turning into sled runs. We were forced to spend most of our time indoors. We didn't like it.

The Hollywood Theater was our only possible rescue from boredom. Located in the middle of downtown Petoskey, it showed the latest feature films and current newsreels. Newsreels were our window to the world outside of Petoskey. People often said newsreels themselves were worth the price of their ticket. The lines that formed at the ticket booth with each marquee change were proof enough. The owner of this communication and entertainment center was also one of Petoskey's most prominent and well-to-do citizens, the mayor. He lived on Pill Hill.

I had an inside view of Pill Hill. I was their paperboy. Paper routes were hard to come by. This gave the newspaper the power to enforce strict delivery rules. I had to cover most of my route in the dark if I wanted to get my papers delivered on time. I wasn't allowed to throw the paper at the house as they do now. I had to walk up and place it on the porch right at the front doorstep. My collections had to be made at certain times on certain days. A single customer complaint could cost me my job. I would have just as soon cut off an arm or leg as let that happen.

Day after day, I saw those well-lit homes. The tables full of steaming food made my mouth water. The beautiful music drifting from the windows completed a scene my kind of boy saw elsewhere only in the Hollywood Theater.

I got in the habit of thinking of myself as someone who belonged on the wrong side of the good life. If it hadn't been for Oakley, I might have gone on thinking like that for a long time to come.

Oakley never was satisfied to be an outsider. He was always doing something to change that. His talents often helped him out, but there was more to Oakley than his talents. Oakley had an air about him that drew people like bees to honey. He was always eager to learn new things and could talk to anyone about anything. People generally left a conversation with him feeling better than when they went into it.

One Saturday morning, the Sheridan Street Rats were standing around downtown when Oakley spotted Mayor Levinson.

"Mayor Levinson!" Oakley called out, surprising the heck out of us.

Even more surprisingly, the mayor turned and grinned. Oakley took off running in his direction. The mayor waited for him to catch up! After a brief conversation, they parted company.

Sparky asked first. "What was that all about?"

"Not much. I just made the deal of the century."

He paused a moment for effect.

"What? What?" we begged him to tell us.

"Well, I know how much we've been wanting to see those movies of his. I also know we sure don't have the money it takes to buy a ticket. So I decided to tell him how much we wanted to see a movie."

"What did he say?" I asked.

"Well, to that he didn't say a word. He just nodded his head. So I asked him if there was any way we could work out some kind of a deal."

Oakley was now walking towards home.

"And?! Can we?"

"'What kind of deal do you have in mind, Oakley?' the mayor asked me.

"'I was wondering if you liked potatoes,' I said.

"'Potatoes? Now just how do you figure my liking potatoes could help you see a movie?'

"'Well, I thought if you liked potatoes we might be able to work out some kind of trade.'

"'I see. So what you're telling me is you don't have any money, but you do have potatoes. How many potatoes do you think a movie ticket is worth?'

"'I don't know. I guess that would be up to you, seeing as you own the tickets.'

"'You're right there. Am I correct in assuming this special deal would also include that group of friends waiting for you?'

"'Yes, sir.'"

We shouted our approval when we heard he had included us.

"'I think three potatoes is a fair price. That is, provided you come by them honestly. Do you get my meaning?'

"'Oh yes, sir. We wouldn't have it any other way.'

"'OK. I think three potatoes a ticket is a fair price. What do you think?'

"I took a deep breath and thought on it for a moment before I agreed.

"'And the potatoes will be obtained lawfully,' the mayor added.

"I nodded, and we shook on it.

"'One more thing, Oakley. This is a very special deal. I can't have everybody knowing about this, or I'll go broke. I'm a business-man after all.'

"'Yes, sir. Just my friends in that group, sir.'

"'OK. This is how we'll work it. You and your friends can come to the back door just before show time. I'll have one of the ushers meet you and collect the potatoes. Oh, and one more thing . . .'

"At this point the mayor paused and carefully looked us all over.

"'I'll make a mark on the outside of the door about up to here,' he said, pointing to a place on his chest. 'Anyone who is taller than the mark has to pay for his ticket in cash. Agreed?'

"'Yes, sir.'

"'OK. It's all set. I'll draw the mark this afternoon. Is tomorrow's matinee soon enough for this deal to begin?'

"'Oh yes, sir.'

"'Good. Now I've got to go. I'm late for a meeting. Good day, Oakley.'

"'Good day, Mr. Mayor. And thank you!'

"'My pleasure, Oakley.'

"'Three potatoes. Don't that beat all!' he chuckled to himself as he hurried on to his meeting."

"That's great," I said. "But where in the world are we going to get all those potatoes?"

Everyone else thought my question was a good one.

"Meet me at Bill's in an hour" was all Oakley would say.

At the appointed time, Oakley arrived.

"Where have you been?" we wanted to know.

"Well, I had a real nice chat with Farmer Thompson. It seems he's in need of some help but doesn't have the money to pay for it. This was just what I wanted to hear. I told him we needed potatoes and why. When he heard about our deal with the mayor he doubled over with laughter. I thought he was making fun of the idea, so I started walking back here. He was laughing so hard he could barely talk, but he managed to call me back. After some haggling, we worked out a deal."

"What kind of deal?" we wanted to know.

"Nothing big. Lawn mowing, filling the cows' water tank, or cleaning out the barn. Stuff like that."

We couldn't have been more excited.

The chores were a snap. We were glad to be able to earn our

own way. Farmer Thompson was glad to get the help he needed. When we finished our part of the bargain, he took us to his root cellar to get the potatoes.

"Pick out three nice-size potatoes. Three a piece will square us for today."

Potatoes in hand, we raced to the Hollywood Theater's alley door. Just before the movie started, an usher opened it. He was holding an old basket. He made sure each of us was under the mark left by the mayor. After we dropped our potatoes in the basket, he let us pass.

Some weeks, Mr. Thompson would give each of us a big, juicy apple. He said that was "to boot." As it turned out, our movie deal was better than we could've imagined. The mayor didn't need our potatoes, but he found a good use for them. In addition to kids, he had a soft spot in his heart for elders. So each week our potatoes would be delivered to those elders who needed them. We earned a good time, and they got a little more for their bellies. Who could ask for a better deal? Without Oakley, none of it would have happened. No one could have asked for a better cousin.

One Saturday afternoon after the weekly show, just as we were leaving the Hollywood Theater, a voice called out, "Oakley! Oakley!" Standing across the street, in front of the theater, stood Mayor Levinson beckoning Oakley to come back. "Wait here for me," said Oakley just as he turned and ran back across the street.

We watched the Mayor and Oakley laugh and talk. After about fifteen minutes Oakley came back to us and here is what he told us.

"Got good news. Mayor Levinson is going to open up the Hollywood Theater every Saturday afternoon for *all* children.

"He did some checking around and found there were many poor kids who never got to see a movie, and not just us Indian kids. The mayor has already ordered a movie, a short subject, and a cartoon for all the children of Petoskey to come and see for free!

"The first cartoon we are going to see is the first one ever made in color. It's about the 'Three Little Pigs.'"

So every Saturday afternoon after that the Hollywood Theater was packed full of howling, cheering kids, all having a good time. I don't think many of them knew that it all came about because of the doings of Oakley. What a guy that Oakley! I often wonder what he could have accomplished if he hadn't got run over by that freight train.

Soon after that, Mr. Les Taylor, who ran both the Temple Theater and the Palace Theater, opened up the Palace Theater on Saturday afternoon for all the children. But Mayor Levinson, not to be out done, gave every child who came to his matinees two B.B. Bats.

How we all loved to see Saturday afternoon come around because for a few hours all the bad things of the depression were forgotten: the hunger, the ragged clothing, the run over shoes. We were just a bunch of cheering kids all having a wonderful Saturday afternoon.

· 11 ·

The Bobsled

The city truck pulled into Henry George's yard towing a 12-person bobsled. The truck stopped and the driver got out. He unhooked the bobsled. Without a word to anyone, he got back into the truck and drove away.

His actions didn't go unnoticed. Many Indians had been watching out of their windows. We rushed outside to inspect every inch of this fine-looking piece of winter sports equipment. We already had plenty of snow. Our spirits were running high, as Christmas was just around the corner. Before long the whole neighborhood surrounded the bobsled. Everyone had something to say.

"I wish we knew who had this sled delivered," my mother said. "It'll be a shame if we can't give them a proper thank-you for such a fine gift."

This was like my mother. She always thought the best about anyone or anything. In all the years I knew her, I never heard her say a malicious or unkind word.

My father was a different story. He took pride in taking everything into consideration. He called it his Scotch nature.

"Could be they're saying, 'Use this on your side of town. Stay away from the East Side,'" he conjectured.

Opinions on this subject were divided, and there were folks who agreed with each of my parents. Either way, we kids were glad to get a bobsled. We couldn't wait to try it out. We had no way of knowing the danger waiting just around the corner.

All the kids, and even the grown-ups, wasted no time in dragging the sled to the top of Sheridan. The giant sloping street made a perfect sled run. We tied clotheslines along the street's sides to help pull the sled back up the hill after a run. On the East Side of town, city trucks did this work for the sledders. Nevertheless, the residents of Hungry Hollow and the surrounding area spent many happy winter nights bobsledding.

Our bobsled run was about three-quarters of a mile long from the top by the highway to the Pennsylvania tracks at its bottom. It wasn't as safe as most runs. Two streets joined Sheridan about two-thirds of the way down. At this point, the bobsled would be going full tilt. The danger came if a car would pull out from one of those side streets just as the bobsled got there. When that happened, everyone on the sled would yell, "Hit the ditch!"

The driver would then steer the sled towards the ditch on the side of the road. We'd brace ourselves as the sled plowed full speed ahead into the waiting snowbank. White fluffy stuff would be flying every which way.

Six times one day we came rumbling down through the hollow. Six times we had to hit the ditch because a car showed up on a side street. It was late afternoon when the sixth near collision happened. That was enough for the girls. They'd had their fill of bumps and thrills for the day. They headed home to get warm and dry.

The rough-and-tumble regulars were still hungry for more action. We brushed ourselves off and trudged back up the hill, pulling the sled behind us. By now it was nearly dark and hard to see.

"Let's make this last run the best of the day!" Flop called out.

Everyone agreed and climbed onto the sled. We were rumbling along at about 30 miles per hour after we passed the first side street, and we were close to the second when, suddenly, headlights appeared. Tired of "hitting the ditch," we decided to try something different. All of us started shouting orders at our bobsled driver.

"Keep going, Archie!" I yelled.

"Go, Archie, go!" someone else hollered.

Everyone, it seemed, had something to say.

Go he did! Unfortunately, the truck went also. It turned right in front of us. It was too late for Archie to turn off the road. We struck the front wheel of the truck head-on. We hit with such force that we knocked the truck sideways off the street. The back end of the bobsled flew up in the air and the whole sled landed upside down on the hood of the truck. The last thing I remember after the initial big jolt is seeing bodies flying everywhere!

When I regained consciousness, I could barely breathe. I opened my eyes and stared into a pitch-black sky. Every part of me hurt. I had cracked ribs and a twisted neck. I could hear moaning, but no one was talking. I propped myself up on my elbow. So much pain surged through me I nearly blacked out again. It took me a few seconds to get a hold of myself. Beside me lay Hermes Otto, face-down in the snow. Rimming his face was a solid circle of blood. I knew I had to get his face out of that blood-soaked snow. I grabbed his hair and shoulder and pulled him over onto his back. That took every ounce of strength I had. Hermes didn't move a muscle. He didn't even know I was there. He was out cold. By this time Hank Dickerson was up on his feet and running in circles around a nearby house. He was talking, but he wasn't making a bit of sense. I saw my brother catch him. He brought him to a stop and made him sit down. Archie, the bobsled driver, had taken the full force of the collision. His leg was in bad shape and bleeding profusely. Sparky had been sitting right behind Archie. He had a terrible head wound.

By now, most of Hungry Hollow had come outside. Everyone was trying to find out who had hurt what and if all were accounted for. The city ambulance pulled up next with its siren blaring. The attendants loaded Archie and Sparky into their ambulance. They took them to the hospital, where they spent the next two weeks. Our parents transported the rest of us to the hospital. Luckily, we were able to be taken home later that evening. There was quite an assort-ment of cuts, bruises, broken noses, and cracked ribs among us.

The Hungry Hollow bobsled run ended that evening. The next day, the city truck came and retrieved the broken bobsled. I watched the truck pull away as I stood at our front window. I knew we were lucky to be alive. I also knew the decision to put an end to the Sheridan Street bobsled run was a good one. As I let the curtain drop, I felt sad. I had to let go of the good times that'd been as close as my front door. I felt a sharp stab of pain in my chest. I took a breath and walked away from the window. The doctor had warned me my cracked ribs would be painful, yet it was hard to sort out what hurt the most.

· 12 ·

Merry Can Christmas

Christmas Eve was upon us before we knew it. Although we were mending nicely from the run-in with the truck, both Flop and I were worried about Christmas. In town, the stores were filled with lots of goodies. It was easy to imagine the joy on our dad's face as he unwrapped a new pair of wool hunting socks. It was easier yet to imagine the smile that would spread across our mother's face as she tried on a beautiful new robe. However, it was nearly impossible to imagine how we would ever have the kind of money needed to purchase such wonderful gifts.

Still, we all did what we could. I continued my paper route, and both Muggs and Flop pitched in to help me. The Christmas decorations on Pill Hill were dazzling. There were big trees with all sorts of fancy lights. Delicate hand-blown ornaments brought over from Europe were hung on the branches and their color sparkled under the Christmas lights. Silver tinsel heavily draped over the trees added even more luster. Most of the trees already had lots of packages under them. They were wrapped in beautiful papers with ribbons and bows tied around them. As beautiful as they were on the outside, I just knew there were wonderful treasures waiting on the inside.

All three of us were drawn to the splendor on the hill. We spent way too much time looking through the picture windows. I liked to imagine decorating such a fine tree. I saw myself carefully unwrapping each ornament and deciding just where to hang it. I thought about the stories each ornament might tell if it were allowed to talk. Imagination was something we had more than enough of to go around. Money was another story.

Our Christmas tree would not be delivered by a horse drawn sled to our front door. If we were going to have a tree, Flop and I would have to get it.

On Christmas Eve afternoon, Flop and I set out for the Russian Swamp. We weren't in the Christmas spirit, because we'd run out of time and excuses. We spotted a small pine tree and decided it would cause us the least amount of work. We made quick work of freeing the tree with our dad's ax and then dragged it home. Next we pulled it into the house and began setting it up.

Dad was standing by the sink washing an empty tin can and gently humming. Neither Flop nor I had seen him do anything like this before. Naturally, we were quite curious. We watched him remove the label and then wash the can thoroughly. Next, he took a soft cloth and began to polish the can. As we watched a bright, shiny finish appear on the can's surface, we asked him over and over what he was doing. He never gave us an answer. He just kept polishing and whistling.

Finally, he stopped to inspect his work. Satisfied the can was as shiny as he could get it, he put it on the counter and disappeared. Flop and I just looked at each other and shrugged. Within a minute or two he was back, carrying a roll of red ribbon that had been in our house for so long neither Flop nor I could remember where it had come from.

"I'll bet it came from the dump," Flop whispered.

I nodded my agreement. The dump was where we had gotten most of the knickknacks in our house. Dad cut a piece of ribbon from the roll and tied it around the can in a bow. He then tied a little card on the can and held it close to his mouth. We saw his lips move, but we couldn't hear what he said. Finally, he wrote something on the card.

"Here! Now you can see what it is," he told us.

We rushed to examine the card. It read:

> Dear Wife,
> This is a can packed full of love. It's all
> I can give you this Christmas.
> > Love,
> > > Dad

What a good idea for a Christmas gift! We bundled up as quickly as we could and headed to the garbage dump. We had Christmas shopping to do!

At the dump we found burned-out Christmas tree bulbs and other unwanted decorations. We collected pieces of ribbon and some bright colored cloth. We also each found a tin can.

Back at home, we tied Christmas tree bulbs on the small pine with string. Next, we hung icicles on the tree. We pretended not to notice they were really strips of tin foil from empty tobacco packs. Hanging pretty colored strips of paper and arranging the cloth under the tree finished our decorating efforts. To us, our tree was as fine a tree as any other in town. Our spirits had begun to brighten, and we got busy cleaning our own cans. The different-colored ribbons we used as decorations made the cans a sight to behold.

Christmas morning came to the hollow the same as everywhere else. The only difference was that ours didn't cost anything. We gathered around our beautiful tree on Christmas morning and opened our presents. The cans of love each of us gave and received were among the finest gifts in town. Mrs. Hoag, who lived two houses away from us, had gotten a big can of baking powder and a bag of flour from relatives as a holiday gift. She shared these things with all her neighbors for as far as it would go. As a special treat, my family drank hot tea and ate Christmas cake. There was no icing on the cake, but everyone agreed there was nothing plain about it. Our house, barely one notch above a tent, was full of the kind of love that lasts a lifetime.

· 13 ·

Good Luck from Hard Coal

Cold temperatures, snow, and more snow spell winter in Petoskey. They also spell hard work and problems. Putting heat into our homes was as difficult as keeping it there. Clothing was hard to come by. Flop and I each had one pair of overalls to call our own. My mother would wash them every night and lay them out to dry. We'd put them on the next morning and try to ignore any damp spots.

After trudging to school, we often discovered parts of our overalls had frozen as stiff as boards. After school, we'd head home under an endless gray sky, with only more chores and cold to face. As one day passed into another, it became harder and harder to believe the sun was still shining above all the gloom.

The day Francis Cooper got hired by the Pennsylvania Railroad, most of Hungry Hollow gathered to celebrate his good fortune. Everyone brought a dish to pass and share. The entire spread didn't amount to much, but the women laid it out on the Coopers' kitchen table as if it did. Most of us were long past hungry when they started. Waiting for them to finish fussing and arranging was hard. We pestered them to hurry and tried our best to sneak a bite here or there to tide us over. We failed miserably. Finally, it was time to thank the Creator for our blessings. Old Frank Michigan did a good job. He mentioned the food, everyone's good health, Francis Cooper's job, William Dunlop and his sons' hunting skills, and of course each other.

As we took our turn through the line, we were especially careful about the portions we each took. It paid off. Everyone made it through with food on his or her plate. The laughter, joking, and carrying on helped to fill our less-than-full bellies. All too soon it was time to step back into the cold, dark night.

"This winter's going to be the worst yet," we told each other as we shivered our way home. We could have saved ourselves some worry if we'd remained focused on what all that sharing had done for us.

Francis Cooper reported to work the next morning and started shoveling coal. Locomotives ran on steam created by heating water in tanks called boilers. Railroads used anthracite coal for this process because it burned long and hot. When a train needed fuel, it was driven under a huge dock and parked. There the coal was shoveled into bins. A side chute would drop and the coal would slide into the waiting tender on the train below.

Coal shovelers weren't given breaks. They had to snatch them. The time during which a side chute was open might be just enough time to wipe your brow or catch a deeper breath. You might even get to rub an aching muscle or two and stretch your back.

Deadlines squeezed a shoveler every which way but loose. No matter how bad the weather or how tired his body, he knew he had to keep working. There were scores of men waiting in the hiring line eager to take his place. Not long before, every shoveler had stood in that same line with the same thoughts and hopes.

The company never discouraged waiting. Openings on the dock were a fact of life. To the man departing the dock, this fact had become a personal tragedy. To those waiting, it delivered a small miracle. The new hire could now provide for his family. The rest of the line hoped they were one man closer to being able to do so.

Miracles didn't happen for everyone, and waiting exacted its own toll.

Will today bring an opening? Do I have time to look elsewhere? Is it supposed to get colder or windier? Is snow expected? How long before someone else's hands or back give out? Will someone slip? Will someone get themselves fired?

If a man was alert, he might detect a slight uneasiness or feel a new edginess plant itself in a dark corner of his mind as one or more of these prickly ideas passed through.

By day's end, if a man did nothing to weed out his newly planted crop of bitter roots, he paid a price. His nerves were strained, his views more cynical, and his heart a little more hardened to hope. Waiting on the edge of survival cuts deep.

Francis Cooper didn't talk as he worked, because he felt it wasted energy. Other men thought the opposite. They talked to keep their minds off the harsh work or cold air. That was OK with Francis. He just kept up his rhythm. They talked. He listened.

The dock's rules were the first thing he caught wind of. Rule number one insisted the bins be shoveled to the point of overflowing. This was to avoid the possibility of a train running out of fuel en route to its next destination. It was expensive and difficult to haul coal to a stranded train. Rule number one always caused some spillage onto the tracks below.

He heard them talking about that spillage. Did they really mean it could be had for the picking? This was hard for him to believe! He felt like running home to spread the word, but he checked himself instead.

No use getting up false hope. Or worse yet, putting the wrong kind of idea out there for somebody to grab hold of.

He checked the area where the coal lay in the snow every chance he got. Two weeks went by. He didn't see a single piece of coal leave the yards except in trains. By the middle of the third week, he decided it had all just been talk. That day his legs felt like lead weights when it was time to go home. He closed his eyes and leaned against one of the bins. Several minutes passed while he mustered enough energy to get himself home. Finally, he took a deep breath, forced himself away from the bin, and opened his eyes. Below him, two men were picking up dark lumps. One man had an empty bucket he flung the coal into, while the other had a cardboard box he was filling. Francis couldn't believe his eyes!

He recognized one of the men, but neither Francis nor the man he knew spoke. The two men below kept their eyes glued to their work. The man Francis had recognized finished first and left the tracks with a bucket full of coal. No one said or did anything to stop him. The second man soon followed with the same results.

What the heck is going on here?

Then it hit him. Payday was not 'til Friday, and homes had to be running low on coal! He knew his was.

Those that knew this black treasure could be had for the picking had generally kept it to themselves. No telling what would happen if word of free coal were to get out.

It was a good thing Hungry Hollow knew how to keep a secret. Thanks to Francis Cooper, this coal was soon helping to heat many of our homes. We were also grateful to the railroad people who decided their trains should be fueled in Petoskey.

Some folks said Francis Cooper shoveled more coal into those bins than he needed to. They said he'd done that to look out for us. Francis Cooper never talked about it. Whether the coal got there by accident or design didn't matter. We often sent up prayers of help for him, especially when the weather turned bad.

A few weeks after Francis Cooper's discovery of coal for the taking, the kind of cold that folks would talk about for years to come settled into Petoskey. Every now and then you'd hear what sounded like a gun report. It was so close to the real thing, you'd find yourself wanting to hit the ground! The old folks called it "Jack Frost pulling nails." As temperatures plummeted at night and rose in the day, the expansion of nails and wood during the day made the two intolerable to each other. The nails would shoot out of the wood with the force of a small explosion. When spring came, Indians all up and down the hollow would be out pounding the nails back in.

No one was alarmed when the cold hit, because everyone knew two things. First, there was free coal lying at the docks. Second, the Sheridan Street Rats were collecting it.

We were glad to be able to help out, but we didn't want our schoolmates to see us gleaning coal along the railroad tracks. Waiting 'til after supper each night solved our problem. Darkness had fallen by then, and few people, if any, would be out and about.

One evening, the temperature was well below zero when Flop and I put on what outdoor gear we had.

"I'm not sure waiting for dark is worth all this," Flop complained.

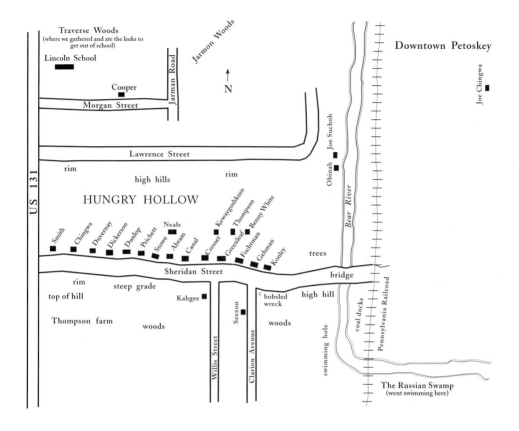

Map of Hungry Hollow as remembered by Bill Dunlop

Several cast members of the pageant *Hiawatha* pose for a picture on opening night. *Rear left,* Mrs. Hattie Kiogima; *rear center,* Mrs. Grace Greenleaf; *rear right,* Jeannetta Walker; *middle, third from left,* Muggs Dunlop; *front, fourth, fifth, and sixth from left,* Archie Kiogima, Bill Dunlop, and Flop Dunlop.

The Dunlop home in later times. The earlier version of the home did not include the enclosed front porch.

William Dunlop, Sr., and William Dunlop, Jr., during the latter part of World War II. President Roosevelt died while Dunlop, Jr., was home on this leave.

"I get your meaning," I said. "After the ridicule B.B. went through because of his shoes, though, I still don't want to chance it though."

"Yeah."

"This stuff isn't supposed to last too long, anyway."

"That's good, 'cause I don't know how much longer I'm going to!"

The cold bit us every step of the way that night. Luckily, black lumps embedded in moonlit snow made our hunting easy. By the time our buckets were full, our hands and feet were numb. The walk home was painful.

My dad had just used the last of our coal to stoke up our fire when we came in the back door. Mother came to greet us.

"Dad, will you look at these two?" she said as she began untying the scarves from around our necks.

"Francis, your face looks like it's been burned. Can you still feel it?"

Flop nodded and wriggled free. He slowly took off his gloves and placed his hands to his face. He could barely bend his fingers. My dad examined his hands. Meanwhile, my mother turned her attention to me.

"And you, Billy! Look at you! You're half frozen. Let me see your hands."

She carefully removed my gloves and gave my hands the once-over. They were so cold I could barely feel her touch.

"Well, Dad, Billy's fingers are stiff, but I don't see any frostbite."

"The same for Francis. Mother, I would say their luck held tonight."

Our parents helped us off with our boots. We sat down by the fire, and each parent took one son and began rubbing his feet to help restore the circulation. Neither Flop nor I complained about the extra attention. We wouldn't have said so, but we both liked it. Dad provided one more treat. He began telling stories of yesteryears.

The knock at our back door was unexpected and weak. Seezon, an old Indian woman rumored to be somewhere between 85 and 90 years old, stood shivering on our back stoop. Many of the older Indians didn't have birth certificates. Seezon only knew she was born the year of a terrible storm. No one could place the year exactly, and she had long ago quit trying.

"Peen-dee-gan" (or "come in"), I told her.

She took off the large bath towel she'd been using as a shawl and bandanna and shook the snow from it outside the door. On her feet she wore a pair of bedroom slippers. Over them she'd wrapped layers of rags. These were her snowshoes.

"I want to see your father, Goosan," she said. (*Goosan* means "grandson.")

"Come in, come in," my father called out as he stood up.

Seezon made her way to the fire and sat down.

"Can I get you some tea?" my mother asked.

She hesitated.

My mother quickly added, "I was just fixing some for myself and Dad. Please, come join us."

Seezon smiled. My mother went to fix the tea, and within a couple of minutes all three were sipping the warming liquid.

When she finished, Seezon put her cup on the floor and stood up. Inside her shawl, she'd tucked three carrots. She walked over to my dad and handed them to him.

"I have three more carrots and a few potatoes at home."

She was telling him she could make soup if she had a piece of meat.

"Bill, run upstairs and bring down one of those porcupine roasts," he ordered.

When I returned, she was ready to leave. I handed her the meat, and my dad signaled for me to go with her. Arm in arm, we slowly walked the half-mile to her home. Her house sat on the side of a hill and had only one entrance. A set of narrow wooden steps was the only way to reach it.

We crunched our way through the snow on the steps and I saw her safely inside. Behind the door, an old scoop shovel was frozen to the wood. I pried it loose and cleaned off her steps before I left.

"It sure was a cold one last night," Archie said as we sat down to eat lunch together the next day at school. "I was glad to get home and stay there."

"Me too, except I ended up going back out."

"Whaaat? Why?"

"Seezon came over, and my dad had me walk her home. Man, her steps were loaded with snow. I don't see how she made it down 'em."

"I'll bet it was hard."

"She doesn't have anybody left to help her out, ya know."

"Yea, that's rough."

"Can you imagine trying to shovel those old steps at her age?"

"She'd never make it."

A few days later, I saw three young Indians up on Seezon's roof fixing her chimney. I smiled and kept on walking.

Flop and I began including Seezon in our nightly coal run. She retired early but would leave a light burning in her window for us. We'd let ourselves in, fill her coal box, and blow the light out as we left.

One night, as we were getting ready to leave the coal yard, I thought I heard someone or something whimpering.

"Did you hear that?" I asked Flop.

"It's too cold too hear anything," he said. "Let's go. I'm tired."

"There it is again. You go on. I'm gonna see what's making that noise."

Flop groaned.

"Go on," I told him. "I won't be long."

My ears led me to some bushes, where I found a small puppy shivering and whimpering in the snow.

I knew I had no business picking him up, but I couldn't help myself. I tucked him inside my coat and walked to Seezon's.

His little heart was thumping wildly against my chest the whole way.

"Don't worry," I told him. "You're gonna be all right now."

Bill, you must be out of your mind tellin' him that. You don't even know if you can find a way to get him through tonight!

I headed to Seezon's, and the glow in her kitchen window told me Flop had gone by without stopping.

I let myself in as quietly as I could and set the bucket down to unload the coal. The bucket had barely touched the floor when the pup wriggled free and jumped from my jacket. I caught him just before he crashed onto the floor, but my quick action scared him. He started whining and yelping. I tried to quiet him, but I was too late. Seezon was stirring.

"What is all this noise, Goosan?" she said as she walked into the kitchen. Her eyes spotted the little pup immediately.

She began making a clicking noise. "What have we here? Where did you get this little one?"

"I found him near the coal."

"Ohhh, Goosan, these are such hard times. What do you plan to do with him? Don't tell me," she said putting her hand to her cheek. "I can see it all over your face. Do you really think your parents can take on any more?"

She spoke the tough question that I'd been thinking every step of the way home.

"He was left to die, Goosan," she said as gently as she could. "Perhaps it would have been better to leave him to his fate."

I looked up at her in horror.

"I know, I know," she countered in response to my look. "My words are harsh, but so are these times. They are much like the hard times of my childhood. Those times, like these, had a name. The *Cleveland Panic* is what they called it. The Indian people suffered then much like now. My parents and many others wanted to return to the woods and take up the old way of life. Sadly, this was not possible. The government people called their idea 'squatting.' They would not allow it, because the land now belonged to the government. There was no food. There was no way to earn money to get it. Many of our people died, and many others were forced to give away their children. Some say we are not far from that now."

Tears came to my eyes. I didn't want to kill this puppy. I wanted to love him! I had been sitting cross-legged holding him in my arms.

He decided he'd had enough of me and squirmed out of my grip. He trotted over to Seezon and began licking her toes. She squealed and moved her foot.

"I can see this one is a charmer," she laughed.

She bent over and addressed the puppy, "See here, little one. I can't save you. I am an old woman, but you have a strong, young friend who wants to try. I will do what I can to help him."

Then she looked at me. "He can stay here tonight. You have to take him tomorrow when you come. Now it's time to say good night."

I felt like the weight of the world had been lifted from my shoulders! I had to find a way to save him. I filled her coal box and went home. Flop was waiting up for me.

"It was a puppy," I told him before he had a chance to ask. "I don't know what I'm going to do. He's at Seezon's for the night."

Flop didn't comment. We went to bed, where he soon fell asleep. I was not so lucky. I wrestled with my conscience and other demons the rest of the night. At 4:00 A.M., I gave up and got up to wait on my dad. I would do whatever I needed to do to save the pup I'd found.

Around 5:00 A.M. my dad came into the kitchen to put on water for his tea. He was more than a little surprised to find me sitting in the dark.

"What are you doing up so early, Chicken Bones?" he asked.

"I've got something to talk to you about."

"I see. Must be serious to roust you out this early. What is it?"

"When Flop and I went to get coal last night, I found a puppy. I guess someone must have left him there to die."

My father knew immediately where I was heading.

"What has gotten into you? There is no way, no way."

"Hold on," I said. "At least hear me out."

He stopped talking and frowned. He was trying to control his Scotch temper.

"Joe takes care of Jim-ta-gu," I said. "He gets all kinds of scraps for free. I can do the same."

"Is that right? And what if you can't? Then what? We have a hard enough time getting food into our own bellies. Every time we go hunting I'm looking at jail. I can't see how you think we can take on a dog, too."

"I don't know how," I said. "I just know I have to try."

That was it. That was all I could say. Dad fixed his tea.

"Where is it now?"

"Seezon kept him last night."

"You asked Seezon?" he started to raise his voice.

"Nooo!" I quickly interjected. "He got out when I took her coal in, and she offered."

"I see. Well, I'll give you one week for this foolishness. If that dog is the first minute of extra trouble, you'll finish what someone else started. Understand?"

I nodded.

"OK, then. Let Seezon know before you head off to school."

He walked over to the window and stared out into the darkness long after he'd finished his tea.

I was now the proud owner of a dog! I was beside myself with joy. I didn't want to think one week, one day, or even one minute ahead.

"Hey Bill," Flop said to me on the way to school that morning. "I got a great name for that pup you found."

"What?"

"Lad," he said with a big grin spreading across his face. "That way everyone will know he's part Scotch."

I laughed out loud at his suggestion. I couldn't help myself. Flop never said much, but when he did, it was usually worth listening to. He knew my father inside and out.

"Lad it will be!" I said as I tried to grab him and ruff up his hair.

He was too quick for me. I chased him all the rest of the way to school.

Flop, Muggs, and I teamed up to take care of Lad's needs. The week passed quickly, and Lad officially joined our family.

Seezon remained a part of our coal run. She never spoke of Lad again, but every now and then I would find a few scraps of meat waiting by the kitchen lamp.

Winter was still in full force, but as far as I was concerned, there wasn't a cloud in the sky. Oakley managed to help a lot of others feel the same way.

The Michigan Maple Block Company ran a sawmill on the Bear River. They made laminated butcher blocks that were shipped all over the world. A lot of scrap wood was produced when they trimmed the ends of those blocks.

Oakley decided to pay them a visit.

"Good morning, ma'am," he said to the company's secretary as he walked into their front office.

She looked up to see a polite, good-looking young man smiling at her. She sat up a little straighter and smiled back. Oakley's smile generally had an impact on folks.

"What can I do for you?" she wanted to know.

"Well, actually, I was wondering if I might have a few minutes of the general manager's time," he said politely.

"You don't say," she said, not bothering to hide the fact she was a little taken aback by this unusual request.

"May I inquire as to the nature of your business?"

"Well, ma'am, I would prefer to keep that between myself and the manager. No offense intended to you, you understand."

"No offense taken. Will you have a seat?"

"Thank you, ma'am. I appreciate your effort."

She disappeared into a hallway, shaking her head as she went.

A few minutes later, she returned and ushered him into the general manager's office.

"My secretary tells me you have something you'd like to discuss with me?"

"Yes sir, I have. You see, I live up in the hollow, and times there are tough."

"Yes, I'm sure they are. Times are tough everywhere. Now what's that got to do with this company?"

"Well, I've heard your company doesn't use all the wood it buys to make the blocks," Oakley said as his voice cracked. His throat was too dry to properly coat his words.

He swallowed hard and went on. " I understand there is some wood left over. Scraps I'd guess you'd call it."

"And if there were, how would that be of interest to you?" the general manager wanted to know.

Oakley looked up and caught the manger's eye directly. "Well, I was hoping, if that's true, you might consider letting Hungry Hollow have some of it for fuel."

The manager told him he would have to take the matter to the officers of the company. Oakley thanked him for his efforts and left. He never mentioned his visit to Michigan Maple to any of us.

Several days later, a truck bearing the company's name drove down Sheridan Street. It was loaded with the company's scrap wood. Without saying a word to anyone, the driver and a helper began to dump a portion of the load of wood into each and every front yard on Sheridan Street. From that day on through the end of the Depression, the dump truck regularly visited Hungry Hollow. Every time the sawmill made enough scrap to fill a dump truck, their driver would deliver it. Everyone was very happy to get the additional fuel. One day, I saw old Mrs. Crossett wiping away her tears and waving a thank-you to the driver as he pulled away from her yard. He, too, was waving and wiping away tears.

· 14 ·

Necessity, the Mother of Invention

Innovation was the bridge to our survival. That winter it also unlocked the doors to a lot of fun and entertainment. Things didn't start out that way, because poverty reared its ugly head. In fact, as we Sheridan Street Rats watched the other kids sliding and skating on Petoskey's snow-covered slopes and frozen ponds, it roared. We knew we had the ability to keep up with those we were watching, but we couldn't afford the equipment we needed to do it. We told ourselves and each other it didn't matter. Fortunately, our fathers didn't believe a word we said.

The turnaround started when Jay Harrington's dad came across an old barrel in the city dump. He got more than a few strange looks as he toted it home, but he wasn't about to let that stop him. He saw more in that old barrel than its scarred and beaten looks showed. He believed he was carrying the makings of a "bump jumper."

When he arrived home he went right to work. He carefully took the barrel apart and began inspecting its staves. He turned them first one way and then another. After several minutes, he selected one and began sanding it. He didn't stop until the finish was as smooth as silk. Next, he cut a two-by-eight-inch piece of wood and angled one end. He cut another piece of wood that he nailed to the angled end of the two-by-eight. This created the seat for his invention. He attached the seat to the sanded barrel stave, between its center and rounded end; the stave formed a runner. He braced these pieces together to give his invention the sturdiness he knew it would need. Finally, he put coat after coat of beeswax on the runner's sanded side.

He called Jay out to his work shed to show him the results of his labor. Jay's face lit up like a Christmas tree. He could hardly believe his eyes!

"It's time to see if this thing works. I'm counting on you for that part," he said, handing his son the "bump jumper."

We all turned out to watch Jay's first trip down the hill. The simple device built by Jay Harrington, Sr., worked and worked well! The "bump jumper" was a hit!

Jay Harrington, Jr., didn't stop with just one test run of his father's invention. He soon became a regular on the slopes. Not much later, the rest of us joined him.

My father took Mr. Harrington's idea one step further. He put toe straps on two of the barrel staves. Flop and I had skis!

The "bump jumper" was too good to stay in Hungry Hollow. Before long, variations of it were showing up all over northern Michigan. The more affluent of the copies replaced the barrel stave with a carved runner that had a smooth steel shoe fastened to its bottom side.

If you are around snow country today, you will still see "bump jumpers" giving their riders as much fun as they gave us that snowy Depression winter. However, kids today don't know they're riding "bump jumpers."

A few years ago, I passed through Vail, Colorado, and stopped to watch the children "bump jumping" down those beautiful mountain slopes. I thought of Mr. Harrington and all the fun his ingenuity brought us. Necessity, the mother of invention, had been hard at work among the Indians. She remained an important part of our little community for the rest of the Depression.

The fun we had from our "bump jumpers" and skis made my nightly coal runs a bit easier. It helped to get my mind off the bitter cold temperatures as January dragged itself into February. I thought a lot about the Kewaygoshkums and their makeshift quarters.

Lillian, their youngest girl, was only six when her family went to the blanket. I thought the cold had to be the greatest hardship they were enduring. Lilly would later let me know I was wrong. Their big army tent had a portion of metal attached to it with a hole for a chimney. This allowed them to use a small wood-burning stove that made the family tent warm and comfortable.

The blizzard that hit in early February, however, nearly did them and Hungry Hollow in. Just after midnight, the howling winds and shaking and rattling of our little house awakened our whole family. My father was already putting on his coat when Flop and I stumbled into our living room.

"You boys get your outdoor gear on. We need to head to the coal yard. From the sound of things, we're in for it," he said.

We didn't waste time asking questions.

"Be careful!" our mother shouted after us as we headed out into the storm. We had a hard time finding the coal yard. We had an even harder time finding the coal. Our hands were our only tools as we dug beneath the mounting snow. Time and again I clawed my way through it only to find bare ground. Somehow we kept going until our buckets were filled. As we headed towards home, I couldn't help but wonder if we had gathered enough to see us through the storm. We stopped at Seezon's but had to shovel our way to her door. A look of relief spread across her face as we reached her door.

"We'll be back to check on you," my father promised after we had filled her coal box.

Back outside, snowdrifts were now waist-deep in many places. We battled our way home while struggling to hold onto our precious cargo. I didn't see any way we could keep my father's promise to Seezon.

The storm threatened everyone and everything in its path. At the Kewaygoshkums', John and Anna exchanged worried glances as the high winds flailed their new home.

Would the seams hold through all of this?

The racket made by their tent's sides flapping in the winds awakened the children. In the midst of all this chaos, John discovered one more piece of bad news. They had no heat! The storm had packed snow down their stove's chimney, rendering it useless.

It was time to take action. John and his sons hurried outside to pile snow as high as they could against the tent's sides. This was not an easy thing to do. With only one shovel among them, the boys had to use their hands to pile snow. John took up the shovel, but it was not much more effective than his sons' hands. The wind blew the snow from it almost as quickly as he scooped it up. In addition, the cold temperatures made the snow hard to pack. Time inched by, and their progress was slow going. They kept at it until they felt they had done all they could. They headed back inside and huddled together to keep warm and prayed. Morning came and the worst of the blizzard had passed. The Kewaygoshkums were cold and hungry, but their home was intact.

Our family huddled together to wait out the storm also. We had heat, but we didn't know from one minute to the next if our little tarpapered house would withstand the winds and snow. It creaked and shook through the rest of the night, making sleep impossible. We, too, sent up many prayers that night.

Thankfully all prayers were answered. Our little house made it through the storm in one piece, and the coal we'd gathered lasted as well. After that, Flop and I made sure we carried home more than we needed for each night. We now knew the value of being prepared.

Putting food on our tables continued to be a challenge. We hunted when we could, but fishing through the ice remained one of the best ways to obtain food in the winter. Back then Little Traverse Bay was unpolluted and still thriving with all kinds of fish good for eating.

Like hunting, fishing also required a license. However, tough times intervened with a twist in our favor. If one got arrested for fishing without a license, that meant the authorities had to feed one more mouth. The cost of food for a prisoner's jail stay easily outranked the price of a fishing license. The authorities became more and more willing to leave us to our fishing as the Depression deepened.

Still, there were dangers involved. These were particularly acute in early winter and early spring when the bay, situated east-to-west, was frozen over but Lake Michigan was free of ice. At these times, fishermen had to be very wary of the wind direction. It usually came from the west, but once in a great while it would shift around to the east. When that happened, fishermen beware! The ice on the bay would be pushed out into the open waters of Lake Michigan.

In early spring, Mob Lawrence, George Sky Eagle, George Green Sky, Ponah Go-Lightly, and my father headed out to go fishing. Each man carried his own supply of hand lines, but they all used the same ice spud. They cut holes for themselves about thirty yards apart and then lowered their lines. Before long, each man had a nice pile of lake perch and whitefish. Plenty of good eating! The men were so excited about the generous catch that day, they stopped paying attention to the wind. It gradually shifted around to the east.

Crack! The terrifying sound snapped them back to reality. They were in danger, and they knew it. The ice began moving towards the open water, steadily breaking into smaller and smaller floes as it went. There was no time to waste gathering equipment or fish. Everyone began running towards the shore, which was now about 150 yards away. They had to leap from one slab of ice to another without falling into the ice-cold waters of the bay. Twenty yards from shore, the ice ran out. The same bay that had just delivered a welcome bounty was now an open-water death trap. Each floe a man stood on continued to move and put more distance between him and shore. They knew they had only one chance to survive. Sky Eagle jumped first. To his surprise and great relief the water was only chest-deep. The rest of the men quickly followed. Shivering violently, they all made it to shore. There was still no time to waste. Soaking wet and freezing, they ran to their separate homes. We kids raced down to the bay in time to see the last of the ice drifting into Lake Michigan. All of us rejoiced that our men had reached shore safely. Other ice fishermen confronted with the same dilemma had not fared as well. They'd been carried out into the deep water never to be seen again.

That night the wind direction changed back to the west. As we stood on shore the next morning, we could hardly believe our eyes. The slabs of ice from the previous day were floating just a few feet from us. The men quickly retrieved their ice spud and their bountiful catch! Their hand lines were gone, but in view of all that'd happened, they considered the loss a small one. We celebrated the first signs of spring by eating a good fish supper.

· 15 ·

Good Talent, Good Times, and Good Friends

The ice in the bay was now history as the soft breezes from the south returned. The snow melted, and the sounds the Indians of Michigan all loved to hear came to their ears. The robins began to sing. Their song declared the long hard winter over. It promised the return of life to all of nature. The wildflowers sprung up, the poplar leaves started singing soothing songs, and the waves in the bay joined the symphony of the woodland music.

Sunlight and warm weather have a way of stirring up something wonderful inside each of us. However, very few have the talent to do anything about it. Oakley did. He was an excellent artist of the paint-and-brush kind. Sometimes it seemed as if Oakley could do anything he set his mind to.

He asked my father if he could have an old overcoat that'd been hanging in our stairwell for years. It was a nice old coat made of a cloth called camel hair. It was a pretty shade of tan.

He turned to my mother and said, "Can I use your old Singer?"

My mother was more than willing to let him. Oakley proceeded to take that old overcoat apart. He cut here and there and then sewed it all back together on her old, foot-pedal machine. When he was done, he held it up for all to see. It was an Ike jacket, waist-length and all. Of course, this was long before Ike Eisenhower was ever heard of or the now famous Ike jacket had been created. It was so attractive it caused people to ask where he had gotten it. One man offered him $25 for the jacket. That was an offer Oakley couldn't refuse. Twenty-five dollars was a small fortune! The next time I saw such a jacket was during World War II, when millions of U.S. soldiers were wearing it.

The best word to use in describing Oakley would be *multi-talented*. It's still a mystery to me how he managed to connect up with so many different folks around Petoskey in so many different ways. John Foley was a good example. He owned Foley's Photo and Art Shop. Darned if Oakley didn't show up one day with a good set of artist's supplies. Mr. Foley had donated the set to him.

"He said it was in recognition of my tremendous talent," Oakley told me, shaking his head and grinning.

To this day I don't know how Mr. Foley got wind of Oakley's talent, but I'm sure glad he did. Not long after that, one of Oakley's paintings caused quite a stir. He called it *The White Stag*. He'd painted an albino deer standing with its front hooves in a small stream. When you looked at that painting, it was clear something had startled that deer. The expression on its face was plain to read. A large full moon outlined the deer and shone upon a stand of evergreen trees close to the water's edge. That picture was so vivid and so lifelike you actually felt an emotion stir within you at your first glimpse of it.

Mrs. Pailthorpe, our school's art teacher, recognized the painting was something special. She started telling everyone she knew about *The White Stag*. She kept insisting they should see it for themselves. Oakley, she proclaimed, was her best student.

"Of course, I taught him everything he knows," she would quickly add.

Oakley never liked people talking about him, especially if it was in front of him.

That day, after Mrs. Pailthorpe had turned to go on about her business, Oakley whispered out of the side of his mouth, "She didn't teach me anything. The Creator was my teacher."

I thought that sounded right to me and told him so. He just laughed.

"She does mean well, Bill. I have to give her that."

With all the interest the painting stirred up, it wasn't long before most folks thought it deserved some special recognition. They decided to hang it in one of the school's hallways with spotlights shining on it. Everyone in Hungry Hollow was bursting with pride over Oakley's accomplishment.

I made it a point to go down that hall as often as I could. I never tired of looking at that deer. One day, Oakley joined me.

"Bill," he said, moving closer to the painting, "I'll be darned if someone hasn't been tampering with the stag. They've changed his eyes!"

"Who would have the nerve to do such a thing?" I blurted out.

Oakley looked at me with raised eyebrows and a look that said, *You're kidding me, right?*

Then it hit me like a ton of bricks.

"Mrs. Pailthorpe! Of course! I guess she just had to let you know she's still your teacher," I said, shaking my head.

Most people would be angry about such an occurrence, but Oakley was more interested in fixing it.

"You're going with me tonight!" he exclaimed.

That was fine with me, because I didn't like anyone tampering with Oakley's painting. Putting that aside, I also knew I'd follow Oakley wherever and whenever he allowed me to.

That evening, Oakley and I set out on our mission. He had his artist supplies tucked under his arm. We waited until it was dark before we started circling the school. We spotted Swede Johnson, the janitor, working in the gym.

"That's our ticket," Oakley whispered while pointing at a door on the side of the furnace room.

"Swede almost always leaves it unlocked. That way, he never has to worry about forgetting his keys," Oakley chuckled.

We waited until Swede had left for the evening before we tried the door. Sure enough, it was unlocked. We slipped inside and quietly made our way through the halls to the painting. While I held a borrowed flashlight, Oakley changed the eyes of his white stag back to the way he'd originally painted them. We retraced our steps to the furnace room, and out the door we went. I felt like we were a couple of thieves in the night, except we were carrying artist things.

The next day, I joined a group of people studying and admiring the painting. I could hardly believe I'd been standing there with flashlight in hand the night before, watching the artist reclaim his work. No one noticed the stag's eyes had been changed. I hoped it would stay that way.

As school wound down that year, so did the excitement over Oakley's painting. My attention naturally turned to the out-of-doors. School started feeling more and more confining.

The last day of May turned out to be an exceptionally warm one. Flop and I were talking in the school yard during recess break.

"I know just where I'd like to be," Flop said.

Closing his eyes, he continued. "Imagine how good the Bear River would feel just about now."

Real quiet like, I said, "I know how we can experience it firsthand."

Flop's eyes popped open and his face lit up like a light switch had been flicked on.

"How?" he said too loudly for my comfort.

"Shhhh!" I warned him.

Then I whispered, "Leeks."

A knowing smile spread across his face.

"Yeah" was all he needed to say.

In those days leeks grew just about everywhere. There were even some growing very conveniently in the woods in back of Lincoln School. When used in soups and the like, they made everything much tastier. When eaten by themselves, they made your breath stink! In fact, the odor was so offensive that if Miss Russell or Miss Wilson caught you eating them, you'd be sent home for the rest of the day. Leeks look a lot like green onions when they're sticking out of the ground. The difference comes when you pull them up. Leeks have a slightly reddish cast that can be easy to miss. However, when you bite into them, you immediately know you've bitten into something really different!

It didn't take us long to slip into the woods and locate our intended snack. Flop and I each ate five of them and returned to class. I took my seat about two-thirds of the way back and waited for the results I knew would come.

I didn't have to wait long. Little Alice Friend came down the aisle and stopped.

"Pee yew!" she shouted. "It really stinks in here."

I looked down to keep from smiling. Alice had done just what I'd hoped she would. She let the whole world know exactly what was on her mind. Miss Russell immediately got up from her chair. She walked brusquely around her desk and then headed down the aisle towards us. She was pointing her nose here and there like a hunting dog.

"Out! Out! Out!" she commanded when she found her prey. "And don't come back until tomorrow!"

I kept my head hung low as I slithered between the desks. I went out into the hallway and through the school doors to freedom! I waited on the corner for Flop. A few minutes later he joined me. Miss Wilson, the teacher of the class two grades ahead of mine, had given Flop his marching orders too.

"Let's go!" Flop said, smiling like the Cheshire Cat.

Away we went at a half trot, heading for the place we called the Russian Swamp. It was really a marshy-type woods on the edge of town. The Bear River bordered one side of it and had a nice sandy bottom there. The privacy of the woods made our swimming hole particularly suitable for skinny-dipping.

When we arrived that afternoon, we found Hank Dickerson and Oakley waiting for us. They had a good-size fire going.

"What's the fire for on a day like this?" Flop wanted to know.

"There's a chicken baking," Hank told us.

"I don't see any chicken," I said.

"It's buried in there. Trust me."

Hank had gotten the chicken from his aunt's hen house. He'd reasoned that he deserved at least one since he did all the work around her chicken yard. Hank and Oakley had dug a small hole and lined it with stones. Next, they put a layer of sand over the stones.

Hank had then gutted the chicken and cut off its feet and head while Oakley had made a trip upstream. He'd returned with a large glob of gray clay, patted the clay down into a flat round piece, and placed it on the layer of sand. Hank had laid the chicken still feathered in the center of the clay. They'd wrapped the sides around it to form a large, gray ball. When they were sure it was sealed on all sides, they'd built a fire over it.

By the time Flop and I arrived, the only thing left to do was have fun. We tore off our clothes and dove off the steep bank. The cold water woke up every inch of our bodies! We wasted no time finding out who could stay underwater the longest and who could swim the farthest. All the things kids do in the water, we did. More than anything, it felt like we were washing out the last remnants of a harsh winter.

Three hours went fast. We knew it was time to eat chicken by how hungry we were! Hank and Oakley scraped the ashes away and uncovered the gray ball. It looked like a big rock. While it was cooling, we got dressed. Hank cracked that ball just like you would crack a large eggshell. When he peeled away the pieces, the feathers came off too. He'd even remembered to bring a little salt from home. Wow! I've never tasted anything better.

As we were leaving the swamp, I asked Hank, "How'd you know to do that chicken?"

"My aunt," he said. "She told me it was the Indian way."

When we got home, our parents assumed we'd been playing baseball at the sandlot. We never said a word to the contrary.

Hank, Oakley, and Flop have all gone on the long walk now. When I think of that fun day in the Russian Swamp, my mouth starts to water over that chicken. My eyes soon join in just thinking about how much I miss my good friends.

· 16 ·

Burnout at Indian Point

June started out as warm and bright as May had ended. It was Saturday. I couldn't wait to get to Frank Greenleaf's back porch.

George Shananquet and his Uncle Fred walked in right behind me. They'd come from Charlevoix to take care of some business and stopped to get their hair cut. Paul Petoskey had just finished telling about some Indians blown adrift while ice fishing on Little Traverse Bay. Fred decided to tell about the burnout of the Indian settlement near Burt Lake, Michigan.

"The dangers of ice fishing don't hold a candle to what happened at Indian Point. Gunfire has a way of getting your attention like nothing else can," he said, snapping his fingers.

"Put a lot of whooping and hollering alongside it and you know you got trouble. Add the long arm of the law leading the pack and you're really sunk. I'll never forget the sight of Sheriff Ming and his gang marching towards our home. Ming generally had a mean streak, but that night he was downright evil. Not much better could be said of that bunch he had with him. Every single one had a look in their eyes that made you question if anyone was home inside. Their guns were pointed to the sky, but as stirred up as they were, it wouldn't have taken much for them to lower their aim."

He paused to give his words time to settle a bit. The low murmurs of the crowd told him he'd hit the mark he was aiming for.

"At the edge of our village, they ordered all the Indians out of their houses. A general sense of panic began to stir among the Indians rousted out.

"'We're taking this land!' Ming shouted at us.

"'You good-for-nothings haven't paid one dime in taxes! That ain't right and we're here to collect once and for all.'

"His gang cheered and fired several rounds from their guns to back up his words. Ming's words were an out-and-out lie. The Indians' homes weren't on the county tax rolls or any other roll. The land had been deeded to them free and clear as a part of one of the earlier treaties. It was supposed to stay that way for as long as they wanted it to. By this time, some of the Indians had gathered their wits about them.

"One of them called out to Ming, 'Sheriff, at least give us some time to get our things out.'

"'You've just been given all the time you're going to get,' Ming shouted back.

"'Now git out of our way. We've got work to do! Come on, boys! Let's go to it!'

"Those who carried torches and kerosene surged forward. They began dousing the nearest home. I could hardly believe what my eyes told me was happening. I kept asking myself over and over one question: Why? Why would anyone want to do such a thing? It didn't take long to spot the answer to my question."

"Did he have a name?" one of the Indians waiting for his turn in Frank's chair wanted to know.

"You can bet he did. And a purpose too. McQuinn was his name, and his business was lumbering. With all the interest the railroad was stirring up for tourists, we Indians figured it wouldn't be long before the white folks would be turning their eyes towards our land. What we didn't figure on was that the lumber companies would want our trees as well. Given all the trouble the white man went to signing the treaties, we thought they'd come for our land with money in their hands. We never dreamed they'd come with guns."

Fred paused and took a drink of water from the glass that had been brought to him. He took a cloth from his back pocket and wiped his forehead.

"The men began dousing all the buildings in the settlement. Every single one was slated for destruction, even the chicken coops and outhouses.

"Helen Waukesha tried to shield her home by standing in front of the door with her arms outstretched. That didn't matter one whit to Ming's bunch. They just doused her right along with her house. One of the sheriff's men threw his torch so close to her it set her clothing on fire. She started screaming and running in circles. The man who'd torched her just turned and went on down the street. Cool as you please, that one was. I guess he thought Helen was just one more thing to torch. Thank goodness young Jonas Midwagon didn't share his opinion. He threw Helen to the ground and wrapped her in his horse blanket. It turns out that blanket was the only thing he managed to grab from his own house before it was set on fire. Helen surely would have burned to death had it not been for young Jonas's quick thinking.

"The next day, only a few blackened pots and pans and one or two flatirons (used for pressing clothes) remained among the smoldering embers. For most of the morning, Helen stood staring at the pile of ashes that had been her home, tears running down her cheeks. Then, without a word, she set out on foot to her brother Tony Foxe's place in Cross Village some 20 miles away.

"Young Jonas spent most of the day wrapped in his ruined blanket. Some tried to coax him from it, but he wouldn't budge.

"'I never want to forget the smell of greed' was all he would say.

"I stuck around long enough to make sure Jonas was going to be OK. Just before suppertime, he got up and threw his blanket on what was left of Helen's house.

"'It's a sad day when a man's greed causes him to dishonor his word,' Jonas said. 'Even if he can get away with it.'

"'You got that right, Jonas,' I told him. Then I added, 'I'm sorry you had to lose that fine blanket.'

"Jonas looked at me and smiled from one corner of his mouth.

"'When I think about what could have happened to Helen, what is one horse blanket? I'm just sorry it wasn't big enough to throw over her house and snuff out those flames as well.'

"No one could disagree with him," Fred said. "Daylight was fading fast, and I decided it was time to follow Helen's lead and make tracks for shelter. I headed to Charlevoix."

A low whistle escaped from one of the Indians who'd been intently listening to Fred's account of the burnout. He added, "That's a long way to walk, Fred. It's gotta be 40 or more miles. Doesn't it?"

"That sounds about right," Fred told him. "But what choice did I have? That's where my relatives were. I did get a ride part of the way on a horse-drawn carriage. Old Magunee had it the worst though. She had turned 106 her last birthday. Don't you know that old woman walked through the woods and over those big hills to Middle Village? That was some 20 miles. For more than half of the way, she had to walk in the rain. When she finally arrived at her sister's, she took to her bed. Heartbroken with grief, she died a few days later. Of course, it's a wonder a woman her age made it at all. They don't make 'em like that anymore.

"There were many people, white and Indian, who were outraged by the burnout. Nothing was ever done to correct it though. Dr. John Reycraft, the owner of Perry Hotel, sent loads of bedding, clothing, cooking utensils, pots and pans, and canned goods to the Indians who'd been burned out.

"During the Blanchard administration, some land was offered to the Indians to replace what had been taken. However, it was swampland and most of it was underwater. No compensation has ever been provided to those Indians to this day."

Fred Shananquet finished his story by saying, "They just took everything we had and then told us it was all God's will."

As Oakley and I left the porch, he could see I was downtrodden.

"I don't think attitudes about Indians have changed all that much since then," I complained.

"Overall, you're right, Cousin," he told me.

"Thank goodness we don't have to live our lives on such a broad horizon."

I shot him a puzzled look. I had no idea what he was talking about.

"Most of the time we have to deal with things and people one at a time. In these cases, the outcome has more to do with you than them," he explained.

I still didn't get his meaning.

"What do you usually do when someone smiles at you?" he asked.

"I smile back."

"Exactly. And when you smile, does that feel better to you than when you frown?"

"Of course."

"When someone smiles at you and coaxes a smile from you, aren't they also encouraging you to find something good in yourself?"

"Yeah."

"And when you're smiling, is it easier to do good things and to have a good time?"

"Of course."

"So there it is," he told me. "If you concentrate on finding that place where someone else stores their goodness, you'll more likely than not see them reach right in and send something good back to you."

"Does that always work?"

"No, of course not, but it works more than you might ever guess it would," he said smiling.

I couldn't help but return his smile. By now we'd reached the tree where Mrs. Greenleaf was just getting ready to start one of her story circles.

"Let's sit down and rest awhile," I suggested.

"You got it, Cousin."

"Today's story is all about something we humans have a terrible struggle with," Mrs. Greenleaf was saying. "It's something that can be a good thing and carry you long distances or that can cost you dearly, sometimes costing even your life."

There was a murmur among the children as they tried their best to guess what this mysterious something could be.

"This is a story of misdirected, or misplaced, pride," she told them.

"The water in the pool made a good mirror. The deer liked to admire his reflection in the water. He especially loved his fine set of antlers. Altogether, he was an outstanding specimen of his kind. His light brown skin had a beautiful sheen that glistened in the sunlight.

"'My skin is really closer to beige,' he told his reflection as he stood admiring himself.

"His muscles rippled under his skin when he moved about. He especially liked to prance around in the herd to show off his beautiful ten-point antlers. There was one thing that troubled this fine-looking fellow. When he stood with his front feet in the water so he could drink, he had to look at his skinny front legs! How he hated them! He detested his knobby knees the worst. In fact, his legs were a great source of shame to him.

"One day when the big buck went down to the pond to get water, he sipped longer than usual. Of course, he took the time to admire his horns between each sip. Suddenly, his head jerked up, his nostrils flared, and his ears pointed.

"Wolves! The all-too-familiar yipping sounds of wolves in pursuit of prey filled his ears. He stood stone-still, listening to determine the direction the wolves were running. Through a gully they went and over the hill next to the clearing that led to the very pond where he stood drinking. They were on his trail! He had to think fast.

"*I'll run through the thicket and over to the clearing on the other side. Once I get there, I'll show those wolves how fast a deer can run!*

"Into the thicket he leapt. He took two bounds, but then, with a jerk, he was brought to a sudden stop. His antlers were caught in the thick brambles. Back and forth he struggled, but his antlers were stuck fast. The yipping was getting louder and louder, and he knew the wolves were closing in.

"*They can't be much more than 50 yards from the pond. It won't take them long to discover I was there and ran into this thicket.*

"Fortunately, deer shed their antlers once a year. Lucky, that is, for the deer. With a mighty yet desperate twist, his antlers came loose. He left them hanging in the branches.

"The wolves were only a few feet away. They were howling excitedly at the thought of the tasty deer meat they would soon be feasting upon. Free of the horns that very nearly got him killed, the deer sped through the clearing with a swiftness he didn't know he had in those skinny legs! Bound by mighty bound, the deer left the wolves far behind."

Mrs. Greenleaf was forced to suspend her story for a few moments as a loud cheer went up from the children gathered around her.

"The deer ran in a wide circle and came back to the pond. His run had made him thirsty. He leaned down to drink and saw the now bareheaded reflection of himself staring back. He realized he'd misplaced his pride. He should have focused on the legs that had carried him to safety. He'd have those legs his whole life. His antlers would continue to be lost once a year. What hurt most of all was that his prized possessions had nearly cost him his life!"

Mrs. Greenleaf was listening to what the children thought the story was telling them as Oakley and I left.

We stopped at home to pick up his paint supplies and a canvas. Oakley decided we should head to the stone bluffs overlooking Little Traverse Bay so he could capture one of Petoskey's beautiful sunsets in paint.

"I learned a valuable lesson from that story," he told me. "How about you?"

I gave him a weak smile and nodded. My head was so full of lessons that the only thing I knew for sure was I needed a rest. Watching Oakley and the sunset would do very nicely indeed.

Roller Skates and Bright Lights

Oakley's system of finding good things in people affected them in special ways. The Indian children loved being around Oakley and got in the habit of following him anywhere and everywhere he went. After awhile, folks got to calling Oakley "the Pied Piper of Hungry Hollow." It was clear to all the parents that their children couldn't pick anyone better to admire. However, even the best role models can't be expected to know exactly where every turn will lead them.

Some businessmen got together and decided Petoskey needed a roller-skating rink. Oakley was one of the first in Hungry Hollow to hear about it and began visiting the construction site. Of course, where he went, the kids followed. Day after day, we trekked to watch the progress on that rink. We were all excited about it.

When the construction work finished, a beautiful outdoor rink, covered by a circus tent, was the results. Admission to this grand arena was 35 cents per adult and 15 cents per child. The admission price allowed its purchaser skating privileges for the entire evening.

We knew that if we were going to be able to purchase a ticket for opening night, we'd have to earn the money ourselves. We didn't mind. We got busy mowing lawns and gathering up rags and old newspapers to sell. We were determined to earn the price of admission to that new rink.

On opening day, ten of us Indian kids stood among the large crowd outside the rink, waiting anxiously to pay our money and get a pair of the clamp-on roller skates. The upbeat "Beer Barrel Polka" blared from the speakers, while the line moved at a snail's pace. We didn't care. We were all yelling back and forth about how much fun we were going to have.

When we reached the stairs leading up to the ticket booth, a man held up his hand and said in a loud voice, "No Indians will be allowed in the rink! You kids turn around and leave."

His words shattered our exuberance. A hushed silence fell over the crowd. I looked around only to find a sea of unfriendly, white faces staring back. We did as we were told. Oakley never said a word and neither did we. We were covered in shame. I thought it might smother the very life out of us. If it hadn't been for a very special gift the Creator sent our way, I believe it would have.

Joe Chingwa, one of our respected elders, worked as a maintenance worker for Petoskey. One day he came to Frank's back porch with exciting news.

"I just got word the city is going to put on a pageant. They've picked the story of Hiawatha and will be hiring every Indian they can find to be in it."

The word *hiring* produced quite a stir among those on the porch. No one had heard of the word *pageant*, and we didn't know what the city wanted to hire us to do.

John Deverney, Sr., was sitting in Frank's chair at the time. He was the first to speak up. "Say, Joe, you can bet I'm interested in anything that has the word *hire* attached to it. But can you tell me what exactly a pageant is? What kind of work is that?"

A general murmur of agreement followed his question.

"Well," Joe began, "I'm not sure I've got all the answers you're looking for. From what I understand, a man by the name of Henry Wadsworth Longfellow wrote about the story of Hiawatha. The city is going to use what he wrote to put on this pageant. I'm told it's like a big play. There's going to be a meeting about it next Tuesday evening at 6:00 in the high-school gym. I hear there's good pay involved and they even want to hire the children."

This last bit of news was really exciting! We talked of little else until Tuesday evening arrived. Nearly every Indian from the entire Petoskey area gathered in the gym at the appointed time.

"Mac" McDonald, the city manager, was the organizer and director of the whole production. He stood in front of the bleachers that had been pulled out to seat us.

"May I have your attention, please!" he called out in a deep and commanding voice. He waited for everyone to stop talking.

"My name is Mac McDonald and I'm the city manager. As you've heard, the city of Petoskey is planning on producing an outdoor pageant using the story of Hiawatha. We hope it'll attract tourists and generate more interest in our community. If we're successful, it should mean more dollars for every single one of us."

With the mention of the possibility of more dollars coming our way, we started applauding. Smiling, he went on.

"More dollars sound pretty good to those of us in city government, too. I've been placed in charge of this whole thing and I'd like to take a few minutes to tell you what we've got planned. First off, each and every participant will be paid for their efforts."

Again applause broke out.

Someone yelled out above the applause, "What kind a pay are you talkin' about?"

Someone else called out, "What the heck is a pageant?"

Mac held up his hands to bring order to the gathering and then waited for things to quiet down again.

"A pageant is a type of grand play. Our pageant is going to tell the story of Hiawatha. It'll be held outside, in the high-school football stadium."

A general murmur of approval went throughout the crowd.

Again someone called out, "The pay. Tell us what you're plannin' on payin' for this pageant."

Mac held up his hand for silence one more time.

"Adults will be paid $5 each and children will get $3.50 each. All pay will be issued after the last performance."

A murmur of shock mixed with excitement went through the crowd. We could hardly believe our ears! This was a huge amount of money!

"Now let me get on with the rest of what I need to tell you about the pageant," Mac said.

"In a pageant, everything is exaggerated. It's hard for me to explain exactly what I mean as I'm standing here, but you'll get my meaning as we get into rehearsal. We'll be meeting here every Tuesday and Thursday from 6:00 to 10:00 P.M. Attendance at practice is required. The pageant itself will take place on two weekends in August. As I said, every adult who attends practices and is in the pageant will receive $5 pay. Every child who does the same will receive $3.50. Each participant will be responsible for getting together his or her own regalia. We want this pageant to be a first-class production, so the city will be happy to provide whatever materials you may need. I'm told some of you will only need to repair what you already have while others will need to start from scratch. I've asked Joe Chingwa to help me out in this department. Please let him know exactly what you need. We'll work together to see that you get it. Summer is just around the corner, so I'd like you to give your lists to Joe by next Tuesday. OK. That's about all I've got for this evening. I'll see everyone back here on Thursday and we'll get started!"

We left the gym filled with hope for a profitable and fun-filled spring and summer.

The women of Hungry Hollow wasted no time getting their supply lists together. Joe meticulously wrote down each and every need. He wanted to make sure there was enough material for blouses and shirts and plenty of beads, sinew, and needles. The planning and preparing of the regalia and props turned out to be more extensive than anyone had imagined. From war clubs and shields to dresses and headdresses, every detail was given careful attention.

It wasn't long before the preparing took on a spirit of enjoyment. Many of us had never learned the traditional dances. Fortunately, there were enough among us who remembered the older ways. They proved to be willing and able teachers.

Our rehearsal schedule was a rigorous one. On Tuesday and Thursday evenings, we gathered in the Petoskey High School gym. The city provided food and drinks for snacks. In the beginning sessions, we children often brought homework to complete.

The first evening, Mac held tryouts for the key parts in the pageant. He started with the narrator, telling us it was the most important part in the entire pageant.

Petoskey had several willing and talented citizens try out. Bill Henry, a city employee and fellow Indian, stood up to take his turn. The very first words out of his mouth told us he was the person Mac was looking for. His fine speaking voice was a surprise to many in the crowd.

Mac didn't make up his mind as quickly as we did. He duly listened to each and every person trying for the part. When the last person had read his lines, he called for a small break and went off by himself to make his decision. When he returned, a buzz of excitement from the crowd greeted him.

"OK, folks. Gather around for a minute."

We did as we were told and things quieted down immediately.

"We've got a lot of talent here. Even though there were several good candidates for the part, I've made my decision. The narrator for Hiawatha will be Bill Henry."

A cheer went up and people hurried to congratulate an embarrassed, but very happy, Bill Henry.

With the tryout for the narrator complete, Mac moved on to his next order of business.

"We are going to tell the story of Hiawatha in two ways," he said.

"First through the voice of our narrator, Bill Henry. But I want you to know, unless you all do your part, the story can't be told. You'll provide the action that brings life to Bill's words."

We still didn't know what we'd be doing, but we were happy to be an important part of the pageant's success.

"Everyone will have to work together," Mac said. "Now let's get started learning how to pantomime the play in accordance with Bill's voice."

We learned that every action was important in a pageant. We also learned that any extra action would only take away from the story that was unfolding. The process of working out what actions told the story in the best way required lots of teamwork. The process was a simple one. Mac would have Bill Henry read a line, or a group of lines if they went together. Then he would select the members of the cast that would be acting those lines out. Sometimes the story called for actions from Indian women or Indian braves or Hiawatha or Mini-ha-ha by herself. He would work with the cast members to decide the exact actions they would be taking. Though simple, the process was also long and tedious. On more than one evening I snoozed through parts that didn't involve me. I wasn't alone. Mac didn't seem to mind our snoozing as long as no one was disrupting the rehearsal itself.

Mac decided to incorporate traditional dancing into the pageant. Some of us thought Foster Otto was the best dancer. Others thought John Kewaygoshkum was better. I personally wouldn't even try to judge them. I haven't seen the likes of these two dancers since those pageant days.

With eagle feathers strapped to his arms and head, Foster Otter was impressive in his regalia. When the drums began to beat, he stepped into the circle and all other motion and noise became stone-still. With his wings spread out their full length, this eagle-man wheeled and swooped around as if at home in the entire sky. The bone whistle he held between his teeth emitted the cry of the eagle and added to the awesome presentation created through his movements.

John Kewaygoshkum was no less a sight to see. The beautiful colors of his Indian clothing whirled and dipped through the arena as he stepped sideways and backwards and turned in circle after circle. Strong and agile, he took command of the noble eagle dance, turning the earth itself into a giant drum beneath his feet. Boom! Boom! Boom! One foot and then the other struck the ground, sending powerful, rhythmic beats flying through the night air. I loved the magic of the sacred eagle dance! My head knew those drumbeats were really coming from the drumming circle, but my heart refused to believe it. I usually joined my heart when I watched the dances. I wanted to savor every moment of those sacred flights for as long as I could. As rehearsals continued, I got up the courage to ask John how he did it.

"Bill," he told me, "the beat of those drums are echoes of the heartbeat of Mother Earth. Just turn your feet over to that beat and you'll be surprised how they will respond."

I decided to try out his advice. During one of the practice sessions for the drummers and dancers, I found a little-noticed corner and tried what John had recommended. It worked! After that, I saw the dances with new eyes. None of them were actually choreographed. By surrendering their feet to the drumbeat, the dancers transformed themselves into the living spirit of the story being told.

Weeks and weeks went by. Slowly, the whole production was beginning to take shape. At the start of each rehearsal, Mac would have the cast run through the part of the story that had already been worked out. He always wrote down exactly who was supposed to be doing what action to what line. Invariably, someone would forget a cue or not do what had been decided upon the week before. Mac was patient with such errors, but he always stopped the rehearsal to make sure the participants learned what they were supposed to be doing.

One evening, we were rehearsing the funeral procession for Mini-ha-ha. Bill Peters, one of our finest dancers, was leading the funeral procession. Four young braves had just hoisted the bier of the dead girl onto their shoulders.

"Hold it! Hold it!" Mac yelled as he walked out to the middle of the gym floor.

At this command, everything stopped. The four young men lowered the funeral bier to the ground. Mac addressed the group of dancers who were supposed to be the mourners.

"Remember, the whole tribe is in mourning for Mini-ha-ha. Everyone—and I mean EVERYONE—has to hold their heads low with faces turned towards the earth. NO EXCEPTIONS! Everybody got that?"

Everyone nodded they did.

"OK. Let's try it again. Places everyone. Drums! Let me hear some drums."

The drumming started up again. It was low and muffled. Hand-held gourds made a soft *swish, swish, swish* sound to add to the mourning effect and help the dancers step in a slow but rhythmic sway. The four young braves hoisted the bier on their shoulders again. The rehearsal continued as the entire tribe moved slowly toward the burial ground.

At this point, the voice of Bill Henry came booming over the PA system, ". . . and so they buried Mini-ha-ha, 'Laughing Waters,' Mini-ha-ha."

On opening night, as expected, all the long hours of practice and hard work paid off. The unexpected happened as we hid among the trees staged on the football field for the opening scene.

The group of poor, half-hungry wretches that had begun rehearsals a few months before had vanished. In their place stood a vibrant, rejoicing, and happy people. Working together and reaching for excellence had transformed us. The pride we felt as young Hiawatha was taught to hunt and then returned as a victorious young brave spread through the entire stadium. The audience was enthralled and celebrated Hiawatha's first deer kill right along with us. Our eyes were opened that night to what our ancestors had always known about themselves. A wave of respect swept through us, washing away our shame as it went.

My father was in the audience for every performance. He told us it was the most remarkable thing he'd ever witnessed.

"People everywhere I could see were openly weeping when the pageant got to Mini-ha-ha's funeral," he said. "I'll never forget it as long as I live."

It was a happy time for me. I felt a deep gratitude for those who had gone before me and helped shape who I was. The pageant restored a sense of hope to our community. My father's words still echo in my ears to this day. I'll never forget it as long as I live either.

· 18 ·

Summer's End

The end of the pageant meant school was just around the corner. I squeezed those thoughts from my mind as I went about my chores. Of course, I had lots of help with my thoughts from a sky that was as blue as I'd ever seen it and a sun that had no clouds to mask its presence. I could smell the bay in the air. Thoughts of my friends and of diving off the city dock drifted across my mind. I liked getting my chores done early. I could always count on the morning sun to warm up my muscles without working them to a full sweat. I set the buckets of water I'd been carrying on our back stoop and took a moment to stretch my back. As if on cue, a slight breeze whisked around the corner and helped me finish off my stretch on its way down the hollow.

Life doesn't get any better than this, I thought to myself as I picked up the buckets and started inside.

Flop came flying out of nowhere and nearly sent me and my morning's efforts sprawling all over the ground. He leaped over me and rolled in a somersault into the yard.

"Doggone it!" I hollered. "Why can't you look before you charge?"

I pried my foot under the door and pulled it open while I waited for the sloshing in the buckets to quiet down. Flop rebounded to his feet, took one of the buckets, and held the door while we both went inside. We deposited our cargo near the sink.

"Why don't we get Hank and Oakley and kick around the dump?" Flop asked.

Before I could answer, he added, "Lots of folks up on Pill Hill have started getting ready to close things down for the summer, and that breeze should keep the flies down. What d'ya say, Bill?"

"Sure. Let's go."

It didn't take long to collect our chums. We headed to the dump, our water-bottle wagon in tow, buzzing to each other about the possible "treasures" we would find. Squealing brakes and a loud thump stopped us in our tracks. As the pained yelping of a dog filled the air, we broke into a run.

I was the first to arrive on the scene. My worst fears had come true. It was Lad! He looked so pitiful lying on the road. My legs were shaking so badly I didn't know if they would carry me another step. The tears streaming down my face blurred my vision as my eyes sought Lad's. He was whimpering. I knelt beside him. He gently licked my hand, trying to get up. His effort failed, and he winced and yelped in pain.

"Shhhh," I told him. "Just stay still. Don't try to move."

A bone in his left hindquarter, clearly broken, was pushing out his skin in an irregular pattern. Once again he tried to get up, with the same results.

This time I tried to be a little sterner. "Lad, you've got to stay put, boy."

I looked around for help, but the car that had hit my dog was long gone. The driver had stepped on the gas, putting as much distance as he could between himself and what had happened.

Oakley organized everyone into a tight circle around Lad. With our hands taking the place of a stretcher, our gang lifted him into our trusty water-bottle wagon.

Pain and suffering made the journey back to our house slow-going. Lad's eyes never stopped pleading for help. His pleas clawed at my heart even though I was doing everything I could. I guess we both knew it might not be enough.

In those days, I always turned to my dad when things got too much for my cronies or me to handle. I took my eyes from Lad long enough to find Flop. He got my meaning instantly and took off running to find our father.

It didn't take long for my dad to respond. He met us not too far from our house. Concern spread all over his face and confirmed my worst fears. In our back yard, my father knelt down and began stroking Lad's head. Talking very softly, he gingerly inspected the injury.

"Let's get him into the house," he ordered.

Again we formed a loose circle to transport him. Once inside, Dad kept stroking Lad's head. Every few seconds a deep sigh would escape my father's lips. The truth was, he'd run out of words for poor Lad. Finally, he stood up and looked me squarely in the eyes. How does a father find the courage to say what he knows will break his son's heart?

Clearing his throat, my dad tried, "Son, Lad has a serious break. We'll have to put him out of his misery."

My father shifted his eyes towards my chums. This was a family matter. No more hints were needed. One by one they patted my shoulder on their way out the door. I knew my father thought putting Lad out of his misery was best. I didn't. I couldn't. I had to find another way or I'd be haunted by those trusting little eyes forever.

My father started to pick up Lad and take him out back. "Francis, get my gun."

As Flop left to do my father's bidding, my brother shot a look of apology to me. I'd never felt so desperate or so determined.

"Wait!" was all I could get out.

My father knelt back down with Lad so I could say my good-byes. I tried. When I knelt beside him, Lad stopped whimpering and began licking my hand.

My brother returned. He was carrying Lad's death sentence. Out of the corner of my eye I could see my mother standing in the doorway with tears running down her face. I knew my father expected me to buck up and face this thing head-on. I knew my father was only doing what he thought needed to be done. I even thought my father was right, but I just couldn't make myself do it. I held onto Lad for all I was worth. No amount of talking would convince me to let go. My father tried every way he could think of to convince me.

He even told me, "We'll get you another puppy."

No words or commands were enough to sway me. Worn out and now a little less sure of his own thinking, he relented.

"Mother, you best make a bed for this fellow beside the stove for tonight," he said, taking the gun from my brother and returning it to its place above the mantel.

Joy leapt in my heart! The impossible had happened! We'd been granted a reprieve. I wasn't sure what tomorrow would bring, but I couldn't think about that now. I'd stood between my dog and death. I could still feel the great beyond lurking over my shoulder.

With our one spare blanket, my mother quickly fashioned a bed for my dog behind the potbellied stove. My dad put Lad on it. Exhausted from his brush with death, he closed his eyes and went right to sleep. I, too, was suddenly overcome with exhaustion. I curled up around him and fell asleep.

It was morning before either one of us stirred. The smell of coffee brewing and the sensation of the air hitting a damp spot on my face interrupted my dreams. Lad was licking my face. I opened my eyes. What a great feeling!

"Good morning to you, too!" I said, nuzzling him with my nose.

I rubbed my eyes and looked around the room. There sat my father, hot tea in hand. He was waiting to have his say. I took a deep breath and sat up.

"He made it through the night," I offered.

"I can see that. One thing can be said for sure. That pup has spunk. I suppose we can try to save him," he began. The joy beaming from my face made him add a quick warning. "Now hold on. Remember, I said 'try.' It won't be easy. It'll be a lot of work. Are you sure you're prepared to take that on?"

"Yes, sir!"

"Even if that means that for all your trying, we still might lose him?"

"At least I'll have tried."

Not entirely convinced, he added, "So you're willing to stay by his side, night and day, for as long as it takes?"

"Yes! From the bottom of my heart, yes."

"Well, let's see if we can rig up a splint for him. Mother, where are those rags you've been saving for your rugs?"

My mother hustled around and brought them to my dad. In the meantime, he sent Flop and I outside to hunt for several strong, straight sticks.

"Go all the way to the swamp to find them, if you have to," he instructed, "but make sure they're long enough to do the trick. Go on now!"

We were back in no time with more than enough suitable candidates for the splint.

"I thought I told you boys to get some sticks for Lad's splint," my dad chuckled, "not lay in all the winter wood."

Flop and I grinned. Dad picked out what he needed and went about setting Lad's broken hindquarter. Lad yelped and cried as dad moved the bone into place. I held him as best I could and wished there was a way to stop his pain. Mom picked up her broom and tried to keep busy by sweeping the floor, but she never moved an inch from where she started. Flop and Muggs sat on the floor in front of us, ready to lend a helping hand if needed.

"Well, that's the best I can do," Dad said, standing up and wiping the sweat from his face. "These next few days are going to be rough. We'll do everything we can, but if that leg gets infected . . . "

His voice dropped off as he realized there was no point in finishing his sentence.

"I know," I jumped in.

I didn't want to hear the rest of that sentence anymore than he wanted to say it.

"I'm going to town for awhile, Mother," he announced.

"Me, too," Flop called out.

I was already lying next to Lad as I heard the door close behind them. He was crying. I remembered my dad's gentle stroking of his head and the calming effect that had had on him. I decided to do the same. My mother came over and pulled up a chair.

"Billy, my grandmother used to tell us about the differences between man and our four-legged friends."

Lad was crying as hard as ever, and I was not too interested in talking. That didn't seem to bother my mother one bit.

"She was very knowledgeable about these things. She taught me four-leggeds do not use words to touch each other, the way we do. They use pictures."

"What do you mean, 'pictures'?"

She answered my question with one of her own. "What pictures are in your head right now?"

"I don't know."

"Close your eyes and tell me what you see," she said softly.

"Do I have to?"

My mother didn't say a word. She just waited for me to close my eyes.

"Oh, all right. All I can see are Lad's eyes."

I quickly opened my eyes because I couldn't stand the pain I'd seen there. My mother wouldn't give up.

"OK," she said patiently. "Now close them again and tell me what else you see."

With a huge sigh, I shut my eyes once more. "Now I can see his splint. Oh, and I can see his leg. I can't see how that splint will really help much."

"So if you and I could send pictures to one another through our thoughts and you were sick, are these the kind of pictures you'd want to get from me?"

I thought back to a time when I'd been sick. Pictures of my mother's smiling face and comforting voice flooded my mind. Lad's whimpering swept the pictures from my mind.

"That's different," I snapped at her. "You're my mother. You're supposed to do those things."

"Do you remember yesterday morning when you were wrestling and playing with Lad in the front yard?" my mother asked, as if I hadn't snapped at her at all.

"Sure," I said, already beginning to feel sorry for being so short-tempered with her.

For just a moment I remembered how much fun we'd had.

"But what has that . . . , " I started to ask and stopped.

Lad was gently licking the back of my hand. The pain that had him whimpering just a few seconds before was seemingly gone. I couldn't believe it! Was it really that simple?

My mother got up and went about her chores. I spent the rest of the day practicing sending Lad all kinds of "good pictures."

I don't know exactly how many days and nights passed before Lad could even attempt to get up, but I rarely left his side. I didn't say much to him or anyone else. I didn't have to. Lad was a natural at reading the pictures I sent him. Once or twice, I think I even got a picture or two he was sending me.

Eventually, Lad was well enough to return to life as usual, although his left hind leg never got completely healed. He could walk on it, but when he ran, he picked that back leg up and carried it.

Dad started calling him "the arithmetic dog." Try as we might, we couldn't figure out the intended riddle.

After lots of coaxing, he gave in and told us. "I call him 'the arithmetic dog' because he puts down three and carries one."

Even Lad broke out in a smile when he heard the meaning behind his new nickname. Lad turned out to be the best dog our family ever had. Many times I heard my father say there was never a better hunting dog than Lad. He was also a constant protector and friend to all of us kids.

Lad loved to try new things. My brother made a harness like he'd seen in a picture of Eskimo dogs. Lad took to pulling our wagon like he'd been doing it all his life. He really seemed to enjoy giving us kids rides.

One time, my mother was feeling brave enough to try a ride. We held Lad still long enough to allow her to get seated. Then we let him go. Away they went! Down through Hungry Hollow, down by the river, down the railroad tracks. And they didn't stop until they got to Crago's Economy Market. They'd been gone a couple of hours when Lad showed up dragging an empty wagon behind him! What had happened to our mother? Just as we were heading out to hunt for her, she came back.

She told us she hadn't been able to get Lad to stop no matter how much she yelled at him. When he had finally stopped on his own, she had hopped off the wagon as quickly as she could.

Mr. A.J. Crago himself had come out of his store and greeted her. "That's some transportation you've got there, Mrs. Dunlop. That dog has more spunk than ten horses."

We all had a good laugh over mom's adventure with Lad, but we could never convince her to try another ride.

"He's got way too much spunk for me" was all she would say as she turned us down time and time again.

Lad's energy was also boundless when it came to hunting. He could run game all day long and never tire. As he ran through the woods wagging his tail with excitement, he would hit his tail against the trees. By the end of the day, both sides of it would be bloody from the lashing it received. In his eagerness to hunt, he never noticed his bloody tail. When we were ready to call it quits for the day, we would have to catch him and force him to stop. He would have run himself to death had we let him.

Sometimes my Dad had to take a small switch and hit him across his rump to let him know the day's hunt was over. Then we'd have to listen to him moaning and whimpering at night because of his sore tail and muscles. In the morning, he'd pop out from behind the stove as if nothing had been wrong. After he and I slept there while he was healing from his broken leg, he continued to bed down there for the rest of his life.

Eventually, we knew trouble was coming for Lad. He'd taken to going hunting by himself. When dogs do that, they start running any kind of game. In northern Michigan, it's against the law for dogs to run deer. One of dad's hunting chums, Hilton Milford, worked for the Emmet County Road Commission. Hilton stopped by one day and said he'd been deep in the Springvale Forest. He'd heard the barking of a hound. A little later, a big buck had jumped across the road, followed by a baying Lad. Hilton told us the game wardens shot on sight any dog they caught running deer.

One day, Lad asked to be let out and I opened the door for him. He bounded up the ravine in front of our house and over the hill.

That was the last we ever saw of our beloved Lad. We knew he'd gone hunting by himself, and when he didn't return, there was only one conclusion to be drawn.

As each day passed with no sign of Lad, my hopes of seeing him come down through the ravine got dimmer and dimmer. Little did I know his passing signaled the beginning of even darker days.

· 19 ·

Dark and Lonely Days

A man wants to be looked up to by his children and wife. He wants to be their protector, breadwinner, role model, and hero! He wants the word *father* to be right up there just slightly less than the word *God*. The day came when my father questioned all of these things in himself. He called it the worst day of his life.

Summer ended and so did the success of our hunting efforts. To make matters worse, there were more and more late-night visitors knocking at our back door. My father had to start turning them away.

One morning there was no breakfast. That wasn't such a terrible thing in my book. After all, the day before, we'd had fish-head soup and that very basic Indian bread called "lud" to eat.

As dinnertime approached, my father busied himself around the yard. No one mentioned it was dinnertime and no one ate. Then suppertime came and went. My stomach was hurting, but I didn't know if it was from hunger or because I was just plain scared. A short time later, I found out it was both.

Later that evening, my father gathered us together. He'd just begun to speak when his voice cracked. He dropped his face in his hands to try to get hold of himself. Then my mother took over.

"Children," she said, "the truth is we have come to the end of all we know to do to put food on our table. We simply have nowhere to turn."

"I'll bet the hunting will get better most any time now," I volunteered. "And until it does, we can just eat fish-head soup."

My mom smiled. "I expect you're right about the hunting, Billy," she said, "but the start of school is just around the corner. Both you and Francis need shoes. And you've grown way too tall for your overalls."

My dad took a deep breath and spoke. "Well, here it is. We have nothing to eat. We have no way to even get the basics you need to start school, let alone to take care of you when it turns cold."

In a softer than usual voice, my mother added, "Let's remember we still have each other."

My parents gathered us around them and we held onto each other for the longest time. It was hard to believe things could be so bad in the midst of what felt so good. We went to bed in silence that night. We were still together, but I had never felt so alone.

The next morning, Father Aubert's automobile turned onto Sheridan Street. As I watched it slowly creep along, I knew where it would stop. I was right. He got out of his car and walked to our front door. He barely had time to knock before my mother greeted him.

"Good morning, Father. Please come in."

My hands flew to my ears. I didn't want to hear anymore. I didn't need to. I'd seen him often enough in recent days and weeks in Hungry Hollow. When Father Aubert paid you a visit, it could only mean one thing. You and your belongings would soon be in his car, headed to "the Convent."

"The Convent" was the name Indians used when referring to the Holy Childhood of Jesus School in Harbor Springs, Michigan. The school sat right on the harbor and presented a pleasing enough appearance. The government paid the bills, but nuns and priests ran the school. Boarding schools on and off reservations had become the government's solution to "the Indian problem." The type of education Indian children got through these schools can best be summed up by the words of one of its superintendents: "The best education for the aborigines of our country is that which inspires them to become producers instead of remaining consumers."

In plain language, that meant the government thought most Indians were lazy by nature and needed to be taught how to work. The government believed that if it educated the "Indian" out of them, Indian children would behave more like white folks. The Holy Childhood School strictly imposed this belief upon its students.

Flop and I took as much time as we could to gather our things and put them in the car. Father Aubert had run into these tactics a time or two before and grew impatient.

"We really must be going," he insisted while hardening the look on his face. His eyebrow started to twitch so much it distorted a good bit of his face. I decided it was time to move things along.

My dad and mother stood in our front yard with their arms around each other waving good-bye as we drove away. I turned away when I spotted the tears that were running down their cheeks. I squeezed my jaws and willed my own tears back inside.

The Convent was only nine miles from Petoskey, but it seemed like nine hundred. Father Aubert did his best to keep his eyes on the road and our minds on what lay ahead of us. He sternly went over each and every rule we would be expected to obey in what he called our "new home." I knew I should pay close attention to his words, but I couldn't. Thoughts of that twitching eyebrow kept getting in my way.

"Above all," he warned, "you are to speak only English. Believe me, you do not want to test the consequences for doing otherwise. Keep these rules in mind and your stay with us will be a pleasant one. Later in life, you may even come to see how we saved you from yourselves."

Flop and I looked at each other. We couldn't imagine why we would need to be saved from ourselves. We thought the school was supposed to be saving us from the Depression. There was one good thing that happened on that trip. My stomach still hurt, but I was no longer hungry.

Sister Zachery was standing in front of the school ready to greet us. Father Aubert parked his car and told us to get out. The old sister cared not one whit what government policy was towards Indians. She could talk fluent Indian. She did so whenever the need arose or when she just plain felt like it. She did this regardless of who was listening.

"Boo Jou," she said to us. "Aaniish ezhiyaayin?"

Neither Flop nor myself moved a muscle to speak. She was asking us how we felt, but Father Aubert had just told us we weren't allowed to speak Indian.

"Ah, I see Father Aubert has been talking to you on the way over from Petoskey. No matter, my little ones. Let's see to your belongings. Why don't you run and collect them from Father Aubert's automobile. I'll wait for you here."

We did as we were told and were soon standing in front of her again.

"Let's begin by introducing ourselves," she said.

"My name is Sister Zachery. Now, what are your names?"

I knew Flop wasn't much for talk, so I spoke up for both of us.

"My name is Bill, and this is my brother, Francis. He mostly goes by 'Flop', though."

"I see," she replied. "Well, it's nice to meet both of you. Here at Holy Childhood we don't use nicknames. You'll have to get used to being called by your given name, Francis," she said, looking directly at Flop.

Neither of us said a word.

"Well, come along, then. It's time to get you settled."

Sister Zachery was in charge of the little boys' dormitory, and both Flop and I were considered little boys. She showed us to our sleeping bunks. Mine was right under a beautiful window. I liked that.

This may not turn out to be as bad as I feared.

In some ways I was right. Many times during fierce thunder and lightning storms, I would see Sister Zachery surrounded by a group of little boys. She would comfort them by cooing to them in Indian just like their own mothers.

Sister Zachery was impressive in other ways as well. For one thing, she had the biggest set of knuckles I'd ever seen. When you're given something unusual like that, I guess it's only natural to put it to good use. Sister Zachery did. She wouldn't hesitate to thump you on the head when she caught you whispering in church, sneaking ahead in line, or breaking any of the many rules at the school. One thump from those gigantic knuckles was all it took to get you back on the straight and narrow.

More important than her strong knuckles, we knew she loved each of us without favoritism. Love was a very precious commodity in that school. That made Sister Zachery all the more valuable to us. It wasn't too long before we grew to love her as well.

Boarding schools are filled with chores demanding to be done. We supplied whatever was demanded. Sometimes that meant helping in the laundry or in the kitchen. Sometimes the walks had to be cleaned. At the beginning of each week, as regular as clockwork, we'd be lined up and assigned chores to complete. One Monday morning, four of us little boys were selected to clean the boys' toilet. We knew where it was located, but we had no idea what was in store for us.

Basements breed a special kind of cold. It's the quiet kind. It reaches out and grabs you between your ribs and then settles down deep into your bones. It lurks between your thoughts and plays with your mind. It lures you into believing you can ignore it. All the while, it's dulling your senses and squeezing out every last drop of your common sense.

We'd just finished our morning meal and were looking forward to the events of the day. We chattered among ourselves as we got out the brooms and mops to do our work. Many boys used that toilet throughout the day, so it was a large and particularly dirty area. We set about cleaning it right away, but the work proved harder and the area bigger than we'd imagined. Silence fell over our group as we concentrated on getting done.

When we had worked about halfway through the toilet area, Victor Carey started looking for a laugh. He started dancing with his broom!

"Look at me!" he proclaimed. "I'm Fred Astaire, and this here is Ginger Rogers."

His efforts worked, because we all burst out laughing.

Archie Kiogima decided to join in the fun, "Oh, who do you think you're kidding, Vic. You need to find somewhere else to dance. Your feet are more clumsy than an old mule's hooves."

Again, we all laughed.

"Enjoy yourself while you can," Archie added. "The only Ginger Rogers you'll ever get to dance with is that old broom you're holding in your arms right now."

That comment brought even more laughter, but we knew it was time to get back to work. It was still dark at that time of year, and half of the basement lights needed to be turned on to finish the cleaning. My brother, anxious to get us back on track, made the biggest blunder of his young life. I'll always believe that cold, damp basement air had a hand in his forgetfulness.

Whatever the cause, I heard him call out, "Ska na badoon!" which in Indian means "Turn on the light."

Those were the last words he spoke in any language for a very long time. A priest came charging out of the dark hall like something from another world.

Robes flying and eyes blazing, he shouted, "Heathen! Heathen!"

He made a beeline for my brother, gripping a horsewhip in his right hand and wildly waving it above his head. There were still many horse-and-buggy carriages and farm horses in those days. But no one carried a horsewhip. You left it in its holder in the wagon. We all knew that much. To our horror, we soon learned a lot more.

That priest kept that horsewhip handy because he was looking for someone to beat up. Pity my poor brother. That priest knocked Flop down and struck him time after time with the ugliest vengeance I have ever seen. The whip whistled as it cut the air. All Flop could do was flail around on the floor. He tried to protect himself, but his small arms were no match for that priest and his instrument of destruction.

Flop's cries were heard throughout the entire building. It seemed as if nothing short of his death would satisfy that priest's lust. He continued to land blow after blow on my brother's helpless body. The rest of us could only stand there and tremble.

I don't remember the exact moment it ended. I do know it was still dark when that priest disappeared. No one made a move for several minutes. I was afraid to even look at Flop. Then I heard it. At first, I thought the sound was coming from some animal, because I would have sworn it wasn't human. Slowly it dawned on me. The strange sounds were coming from Flop!

He wasn't crying. He was hurt too badly to do that. His tiny bit of whimpering had an eerie, high-pitched edge to it. I went over and knelt beside him.

"Flop," I whispered.

The sound of my voice caused him to recoil in fear. The quivering mass that lay before me was only a shell. I had no idea where the Flop I knew had gone or how to coax him back. I didn't even know if I wanted to try.

You gotta at least try, a little voice inside me urged. *Go on. You can't wait or it'll be too late.*

"It's Bill." I said out loud. "Your brother, Bill."

Flop didn't move. Flop needed help. We had to move him. I was afraid that if I touched him, I'd cause him to die right there on the basement floor.

The voice came back to urge me on. *Move him. You've got to get him out of here. NOW!*

"Flop, we have to get you out of here," I told him. "I know it's going to hurt, but we can't let you stay here."

Tears were pouring down my face. "Don't you die on me," I told his limp little body. "I mean it. Don't you dare die on me!"

We carried Flop to the little boys' dormitory and put him to bed. His entire body was bruised. Raised welts crossed his body. I sat down beside his bed and put my hand as close as I could get it to him without touching him. I lowered my head and felt myself sink into despair. I couldn't stay by his side, because school rules wouldn't permit it.

Through many meals, Flop wasn't strong enough to come down and march to eat with the rest of us. Even though horse corn, cauliflower, and an occasional roadkill might not sound too appetizing by today's standards, back then it was all that stood between us and hunger and we welcomed it. However, school rules said if you couldn't get to meals, you didn't need to eat, and that meant Flop should have gone hungry.

Archie, Victor, and myself decided otherwise. Where we got

the strength to make such a decision, given what we'd been through, I'll never know. I like to think the Creator gave it to us, but that's me. I do know I was grateful to receive it.

At each meal, we hid part of our food under our shirts and carried it up to Flop. Lucky for us, we didn't get caught. If we had, we knew that priest was always ready and eager to find a new prey for his whip.

The police never came to investigate Flop's beating, because no one ever called them, not even Sister Zachery. In fact, no one ever reported the many beatings that happened to boys and girls alike. We never knew why. We just knew no one except that priest himself was safe from that terrible wrath.

Visits to the Convent were both hard for and hard on my parents. The first part of their difficulty was brought on by their lack of transportation. It was the second part that took the greatest toll on them, but it would be several more years before I really understood why.

They were always on the lookout for a way to get to Holy Childhood for a visit. Every once in awhile, their vigilance and a little bit of luck would make it happen. Of course, that meant we never knew from one visit to the next when we might see them again. We had to accept the way things were and we did. We just never liked it.

A few weeks after Flop's beating, he and I were playing outside when we saw them walking towards us. They were all smiles.

My heart leapt for joy. We ran to greet them, but a prickly feeling overtook me before we got to them. I slowed down just a bit to give myself time to shake it off. The last thing I wanted to do was spoil our visit together.

"Will you look at these two?" I heard my mother exclaim to my father.

She held out her arms waiting to encircle us in a hug. "I swear you boys have grown an inch or maybe two since our last visit."

I decided it was best to let Flop go first. He was more than happy to. As they embraced, her eyes caught mine for a brief moment. She didn't say a word but released Flop and reached out to me. After a quick hug, she took my face in both her hands and looked at me to see if she could read what was troubling my heart.

She dropped her hands and said, "Are you boys hungry? Dad and I brought a little something to share with you for dinner. That is, if you're interested."

Our shouts of glee answered her completely. We found a place to share what they had brought and for the briefest of moments things felt like old times. We didn't talk much. I don't know why exactly. I think we mostly wanted to take in the feelings of being together right along with each and every bite of food we ate. Much too soon it was time for them to head back home.

This time it was my father who spoke. "You boys have been awful quiet this visit. Have things been goin' OK?"

Flop and I looked at each other and then at my father. We knew he expected the truth from us. So, we told him. When we had finished, a heavy silence hung in the air.

My father drew in a deep breath and let it out slowly. "I appreciate your honesty."

He looked at Flop. "I can't do anything to take back what happened to you. What's done is done. I can tell you I don't like it one little bit and I'm truly sorry you had to go through that. What that man did to you was just plain wrong. Being a priest and all, he should know better."

The anger rising up in my father was plain to see. My mother gently put a hand on his elbow to stop what might get out of hand.

"It's all right, mother," he told her. "I'm not about to do something foolish, although I don't mind telling you I'd sure like to."

"Bill," he told me, "I'm proud of what you did for your brother."

Then it was Flop's turn again. "I'm proud of you, too, son."

His next words closed the subject between us forever. "One good thing this awful mess tells me is that I can count on you two to look out for one another. I want you to know that's no small thing. I also want you to know I'm going to get you out of here just as soon as I can. You have my solemn word on that."

There was only enough time for a quick hug before they were on their way. Flop and I stood with our arms around each other, waving, until they were out of sight. As we turned and started back towards Holy Childhood, I realized that prickly feeling had disappeared. I was glad.

Archie, Victor, and I are old men now. We still see each other from time to time at Ghost Suppers, senior luncheons, and the like. Ghost Suppers are very important to the Indian people. They are a traditional gathering to remember with prayers, singing, and feasting, the loved ones who have died. The spirits are always fed with the first plate of food from the feast and one empty chair is left for them at the table. Ghost Suppers also provide an opportunity to visit old friends, eat Indian food, catch up on "Indian news," talk over problems, learn from each other and put away loneliness. Occasionally, our talk turns to Holy Childhood and Flop's beating.

One of us always says something like "I wish that old B-st—d would try it now!"

Of course, we know nothing like that will ever happen. That priest went on to his reward many years ago. Flop has gone on to his as well. He never got over the bitterness that encounter with that priest caused him and neither have I.

Sister Zachery is a different story, in my book. It took me awhile and a whole lot more living before I came to understand that the most important part of a person's life is the love and kindness they show, not the mistakes they make along the way. I'll never forget her kindness if I live to be 100 years old. I'm not the only one who feels this way.

I have attended two huge funerals in my life. One was Sister Zachery's and the other was that of Chief Ike Peters. The cortege for each of them stretched as far as the eye could see. I saw many eyes that were as red as mine when we said good-bye to that kind old lady. God bless you, and che megwetch, Sister Zachery, for everything you did and for everything you taught me.

· 20 ·

Homecoming

I was homesick the whole time we were at the Convent, even though our little house in Hungry Hollow wasn't much better than the Kewaygoshkums' tent. Our house hadn't been painted in years, and almost all the windows were cracked and patched. The linoleum flooring was worn bare, and there was no money to replace it. None of the furniture matched. It had all been gathered from here and there. Some of it had even come from the city dump.

My mother had made all of our blankets herself from old overcoats. Some of the blankets still had the overcoats' pockets on them. When Flop wanted to keep something from me, he would put it in one of those pockets.

By most standards it wasn't much of a home, but to Flop and me it was everything we ever wanted and then some. I felt safe and secure with my big, strong dad around. My mother served very simple food, but the amount of love and caring she poured into her cooking always made our meals tasty. I missed both of them terribly.

Our parents missed us, too. They came to visit us every weekend they could find a way to get there. When it was time for them to return to Hungry Hollow, there were always lots of hugs and usually some tears. I would run all the way up to the dormitory and climb on my bed. If I stretched onto the tips of my toes, I could get my nose level with the window that looked out over the harbor. I'd watch them make their way back home for as long as the muscles in my arms and legs would hold out. Exhausted, I'd finally have to give up. I'd drop to my bed and wait. A heavy, black cloud of despair always closed in around me after they were gone. We were a family, and more than anything else in the world, we wanted to live like one again.

The winter that year was long and harsh. I was more than ready when the buds on the trees appeared and the first robins arrived from the south. The news we'd been hoping and praying for blew in right behind the robins.

My father had found work! He'd been hired by McManus Sawmill as a lumberjack. More specifically, they hired him to do log burling. In the world of lumberjacks, log burling is a specialty that requires agility, skill, and quick thinking. My father excelled in all three.

Logs were floated to a holding pond before they entered the sawmill for processing. There, log burlers would jump onto the logs and guide them through the water by rolling them, moving from log to log. It was not only physically demanding but also very dangerous.

The day the sawmill hired my father, he felt his manhood had been restored. He never thought of the work as tedious, nor did he worry about the dangers involved.

"To me, it's like being asked to dance to the music of a thousand bagpipes and being paid to boot." That was the answer he always gave when or if someone expressed concern about his work.

My parents immediately contacted the Convent to see when we could come home. Father Aubert advised them to wait until the end of the school term. Reluctantly, they acknowledged the wisdom of his advice and agreed to follow it. The news of my father's new job soon spread through the hollow. When it reached the ears of Mrs. Milford, she wasted no time before making a visit to my parents. She offered her Model A Ford as the transportation to bring us home.

Kids today talk about "joyriding" in their cars as a form of recreation. That spring morning when we packed our belongings and headed back to Hungry Hollow was my first taste of "joyriding." It was the best time I've ever had in an automobile. Nothing since has ever come close to that beautiful feeling of going just where you wanted to go, with all of your loved ones, and in style to boot! Even more surprises awaited us at home.

Oakley had joined our family. His father had died, and his

mother had remarried and moved to Kewadin. His new stepfather did not really like the idea of taking on a ready-made family. The day after my father was hired to work at the sawmill, Oakley had hitch-hiked back to Petoskey to ask my parents if he could stay with them. In those days, the Indian people were still following the old ways. When a child needed a new home or family, they didn't go through an adoption agency or the courts. They just took the child as their own and that was that. Benny White was taken in by John and Jane White, and he was, ever after, one of us. Evelyn Kewandaway came into our lives one day, and out of the blue she was a little sister to all of us. Many years later, Flop would continue this tradition by taking four boys as his own. All four grew up to be really fine men and good citizens.

So it was with Oakley and our family. He just showed up from Kewadin, stated his need, and from then on was a part of our family. Before the Europeans came, the Indian child belonged to the whole band. There were no unwanted, unloved orphans. They were taught everything they needed to know by all the elders and done so lov-ingly. Should a man be killed somehow or die of sickness, his imme-diate family members were not considered a widow and orphans left behind to be a burden on someone. They were just accepted and loved by all. That, we were told, was the Indian way. That was OK with me, because it meant something good for Oakley.

Oakley and I began spending more and more time together. We no longer made excuses for going to listen to Mrs. Greenleaf's sto-ries. We would walk to within 10 yards of the circle of kids and sit on the grass.

One day, Oakley nudged me with his elbow and said, "Look at Mose Redbird and Jake Greensky over there waiting for one of Frank's haircuts. Do you think they really need to be that close to the kids' circle? You see Johnny Mixamong over there leaning on that fence post?"

I nodded and grinned. We all wanted to hear Mrs. Greenleaf's stories. None of us wanted to appear childish, and little games gave many the vehicle to listen free of worry.

Oakley took a piece of candy out of his pocket. I didn't even have to look at it to know it was a B.B. Bat. At two for a penny, it was his favorite and the only kind he ever ate. When he popped it into his mouth, the big voice of Mrs. Greenleaf boomed out, "Oakley Bush, we don't eat during our story time!"

"Yes, ma'am!"

Oakley quickly put it back in his pocket, and like it or not, Mrs. Greenleaf had made us a part of her learning circle.

I didn't know a "redskin" could blush, but Oakley's beet-red face showed me that one could indeed.

Mrs. Greenleaf paid Oakley no further mind and began her story. "You all knew Mrs. Smith's dog, Buster, didn't you?"

A few of the children acknowledged they had known Buster, and a few admitted they had not.

"Mary Smith had a dog named Buster. Together they lived on the hill above Hungry Hollow," Mrs. Greenleaf explained. "The dog was a collie-spaniel mix. He had a regal bearing about him. Even on the hottest summer days, he would trot along with his head held high, as he made his daily trip down Sheridan Street to the Bear River. Once there, he would take a swim to cool off, and then he would make his return trip in the same manner. He certainly was something special. If you called out his name, he would turn his head to look at you and smile."

Several of the children exchanged questioning glances. Nothing escaped Mrs. Greenleaf's sharp eyes.

"Yes, you children heard me correctly. I said 'smile' and I meant it. There are very few dogs that can do that. Perhaps, when you walk these roads as long as I have, you will be fortunate enough to come across a smiling dog for yourself one day. Until then, you'll just have to take my word for it."

Everyone quickly nodded their willingness to do so. They had no desire to offend Mrs. Greenleaf in any way.

She smiled and went on. "Fern Coon acquired a small dog somewhere, and before long that dog took to harassing Buster as he trotted by. He would run out and yip and snap at Buster's legs. Old Buster paid the cur no mind. He'd just keep on high-stepping down the road.

"One day, the cur made the mistake of his life. He took hold of Buster's leg with his teeth! What happened next was too fast for the eye to follow. In a flash, Buster grabbed the cur and, with one flip of his head, sent the foolish dog rolling end over end. When he stopped rolling, the cur ran to his backyard crying, 'Ki yi Ki ying.' Never again did Buster have to put up with that other dog's harassing. When that cur of Fern Coon's saw Buster trotting down through Hungry Hollow, he'd run fast as he could to his own backyard and peek around the corner until Buster was safely out of sight. Now what do we learn from this little story about the two dogs?"

Mrs. Greenleaf waited for the answers to come.

One little boy volunteered, "Let sleeping dogs lie."

A little girl said, "There are different kinds of dogs."

Finally, one of the older children said, "When a dog is trotting by, let that dog trot on by and mind your own business."

"That's close enough," Mrs. Greenleaf said.

Oakley signaled me it was time to go. Jake Greensky and Mose Redbird decided it was time for their haircut and headed into Frank's back porch.

· 21 ·

WPA to the Rescue

Things started happening in Washington, DC, that would bring a wonderful change to northern Michigan. Important news like that travels fast in Indian country. One morning, not too long after the sun had come up, we heard the familiar voice of Melvin Stowe, Hungry Hollow's "news spreader," coming down the street. Hungry Hollow had no phones and only one radio. Nobody could afford a newspaper. So the way we got big news was from people like the town criers of olden times.

Melvin's wasn't a paid position; yet he was Hungry Hollow's first, and sometimes only, link to what was happening in the world. Melvin was neither appointed nor elected. He simply took it upon himself to provide this much-needed service to his friends and neighbors. No one could have done it any better. Old Ellory tried to do it once when Italy attacked Ethiopia in 1938, but he got everything all mixed up. He came through the hollow bellowing, "War is coming! The Italians are fighting Italy."

You could always count on Melvin to get the news right. "There's big news out of Washington!" he called out on his way by. "It's gonna mean better times for sure. It's all over the radio. Frank's got his on and says anyone who's interested is welcome to hear for themselves."

Brief and to the point was Melvin's style. We waved our thanks to him as he continued on his way up the hill. No one ever talked to Melvin when he was making his rounds. We all knew better. To talk to him or ask questions would only delay him and then delay others from receiving the same news. No one wanted to be that rude or inconsiderate. Instead, we all hurried down to Frank's.

A new government work program was being started. It was part of something President Franklin D. Roosevelt was calling the New Deal. The part of the New Deal that interested us was the WPA. There had been a work program tried before, but it hadn't done us any good, because it had required a person to already have a job to qualify for it. Since most of us didn't have jobs, the program had done us no good.

The WPA was different. It was for anyone who needed a job and wanted to work. There were no restrictions. Race didn't matter, lack of education was no barrier, and you needed no experience to qualify. The only requirement was that you wanted to work. The pay was only $1.88 a day. However, to those who had been struggling along with no pay at all, it was heaven-sent! It meant they could now afford the basics, such as flour, sugar, salt, and baking powder, and once in a great while, a little piece of meat!

John Kewaygoshkum came walking up to our house.

First thing he said was, "Have you heard about this WPA? Do you really think it's coming here?"

My father responded, "John, I'm of a mind I'll have to see it to believe it, but I sure do hope so."

We didn't have to wait long. About a month later, anyone in Hungry Hollow who wanted to was working. The result of all those jobs was soon apparent. The holes in everyone's shoes and in the seats of their pants disappeared. The kids now had schoolbooks. Of course, they were secondhand, but the words printed in their books were just as readable as in the brand new ones. Birthday parties started happening again.

That summer proved to be the last the Kewaygoshkum family would spend in their bayside camp. All in all, the devastation and hardship of the fire had turned into a great time for the kids—all nine of them! Hershel, the youngest boy, told me he loved every minute there. He had the beach at his back door. He loved to listen to the waves and the sound of the poplar trees. He said the food and even the water tasted much better while they were there.

The Kewaygoshkum family ordeal had a happy ending. They found a vacant house to rent about a half-mile down the road from their camp, towards town, and fixed it up in no time at all. All the Kewaygoshkums were happy they didn't have to leave the beach they'd come to love. The thing John and Anna were most happy about was that their children all came through in robust health. There wasn't a sickly one among them. They'd even started attending Mrs. Greenleaf's circles again.

I was surprised to see them there for the first time in a long while. I was even more surprised when I heard Mrs. Greenleaf use my father's name that day.

She said, "Bill Dunlop, Sr., told my husband and myself about this encounter with a very smart fox. While he was out hunting one day, he encountered a small hill. Deciding to see what was on the other side, he began climbing it until he got to the point where his eyes were high enough to look over the top. He spotted a fox trotting along. Mr. Dunlop knew that fox was headed straight for a baited trap! He waited to see how the fox would handle the situation.

"The fox stopped suddenly and froze statue-still. It seems he'd caught the scent of the trap. With his nose twitching, he walked very slowly until he spotted what he'd smelled. Then, ever so slowly, he circled around it. Next, he approached it with his neck outstretched and his nose working. Then, he drew back and again circled the trap. The fox kept this up until he had approached the trap from all four directions. He finally decided he'd had enough. His senses and instincts told him this was set by a man in order to catch some dumb fox. Well, it wouldn't be this fox that would get trapped by those steel jaws! Then, just to help some animal not quite as smart as he, and to let the trapper know his trick didn't work, the fox coughed several times and spit on the trap. He kept coughing and spitting until the entire trap was covered. Mr. Dunlop told us he saw a look come across the fox's face that suggested he was getting a lot of enjoyment from his work. Without so much as a glance backwards, the fox haughtily trotted away."

Mrs. Greenleaf stuck her nose in the air and brushed her hands off several times, imitating the haughty attitude of the fox. She didn't look much like a fox, but she was funny. We all laughed.

"Now children," said Mrs. Greenleaf, "what do we learn from this smart little fox?"

"Look before you leap," called out one little boy.

"All that glitters is not gold," called out another.

"Don't judge a book by its cover!" shouted Oakley. He made a face and clapped his hand over his mouth, embarrassed by his enthusiasm.

Mrs. Greenleaf took this in stride just like she did everything that came her way. "All of you are partly correct. What we learn from this lesson is that when something looks too good to be true, that means it usually is. We need to always check these things out."

Oakley, still looking sheepish, whispered out of the side of his mouth, "Let's get out of here. People will start talking about us enjoying these little tikes' gatherings too much."

Down the road, Oakley took out his "chromatic" and said, "I want to teach you how to tell when a musician is modulating to a different key."

I perked up and paid close attention to what he was telling me. I wanted him to know I still looked up to him, in spite of what he considered a childish outburst. He continued on as if nothing had happened. Oakley had regained his composure, but with a self-imposed price. That was the last time we ever attended one of Mrs. Greenleaf's meetings.

· 22 ·

From Boy Scouts to Jail

Two men dressed in business suits, white shirts, and ties pulled their car over and parked across the street from Sam Abram's house. Faces quickly appeared in the windows of his neighbors. They wondered who these men were and what they were doing in Hungry Hollow.

When Oakley and I came along, we were surprised to see John Foley getting out of the car. We waved and walked over to say hello.

"Hello, Mr. Foley," Oakley called out. "I've been giving those paints quite a workout."

"So I've heard. One of my customers was going on and on about a sunset you painted out at the lime pit. Couldn't stop talking about it."

When we reached his car, Oakley introduced me. "Mr. Foley, this is my cousin, Bill Dunlop."

"Nice to meet you," he said, extending his hand to me.

"Nice to meet you," I said, shaking his hand.

"Bill and Oakley, I'd like you to meet a friend of mine. This is Mr. Chamberlain."

"Hello," we said in unison.

Mr. Foley continued, "Wayne is in the insurance business, and we both are members of the Kiwanis club. The fact is, Oakley, you have something to do with the reason we've come to call today."

Oakley and I looked at each other with puzzled looks.

"Let me explain. That *White Stag* painting of yours has caused quite a stir among folks in Petoskey. Why, we'd no idea there was such a talented young man in our area. At our last Kiwanis meeting, we were all remarking how wonderful your painting is. The question occurred to us, Who knows how many talented young men might be in Hungry Hollow? My friend Wayne, here, had the idea of forming an Indian Boy Scout troop for all the Indian boys in these parts. Boy scouting can bring about a lot of opportunities, you know. Everyone thought that was a great idea. Wayne and I volunteered to find out what you boys might think of it. If you like the idea, there is a whole group of businessmen who'd be willing to sponsor such a troop."

Neither Oakley nor I said a word.

He went on. "We've already contacted Chief Joe Chingwa about this, and he's agreed to accept the appointment of scout-master."

"I think that's a great idea!" I volunteered immediately.

To my surprise, Oakley only said, "That sounds like a very generous offer, but I'd like to know a little more about what all it involves."

"Of course," Mr. Foley said. "Boy scouting takes a definite commitment."

We shook hands and went on down to Bear River. Mr. Foley and Mr. Chamberlain went door to door presenting their offer to the boys of Hungry Hollow. Oakley wasn't at all enthused about it.

He told me, "I don't know what to make about this. I'm not sure I like them tying this idea up to my painting. They haven't cared two dead flies' worth about us Indians before. On the other hand, Mr. Foley has been nothing but great to me. I don't know, Bill. I just don't know."

Oakley was like wauksha, which is the Indian word for fox. (By that we meant he was suspicious about anything suddenly offered to us.) Most of the other Indians were all for the scout troop. They liked the opportunity we'd be given to work a few hours a week to earn our uniforms and a little spending money.

Many of us joined up. Henry Dickerson was the luckiest among us as far as jobs went. He got to work helping to clean the Temple Theater and got a bonus of a free show now and then.

The scout troop turned out to be one of the best things that ever came our way. Our scout uniforms were the finest clothes any of us had ever worn. When we put them on, we always felt we'd taken quite a step up. We did a lot of fun and exciting things in our meetings.

Leo "the Turtle" Meshekey taught us a military drill. We took to it like ducks to water. Little did we know our drilling was a dress rehearsal for the war that loomed ahead of us. We didn't worry much about conquerors coming our way. What could anyone possibly want with anything we had?

Our meetings were held once a week. We learned to tie knots, make leather goods, and do other kinds of crafty things. We earned merit badges for doing this. One thing they didn't need to teach us was woodsmanship. In fact, if we had been less polite, we probably could have taught them a thing or two.

We must have been a pretty tough bunch of boys. Early that next spring, Mr. Chamberlain took us to his cabin on Pickerel Lake. The air was still quite nippy, and a ring of ice edged the lake. We could have cared less. We were so excited to be on the outing, we just ran, jumped over the ice, and went swimming!

Marching in all the parades was another perk we enjoyed. We were good in precision drill and got many rounds of applause as we went singing by. I can still see the proud look on John Duvernay's face as he carried the American flag. The men of the Kiwanis club helped us much more than they could have possibly known.

I guess Hermes Otto summed it up pretty good when he said, "The best thing I learned is we're just as darned good as anyone else. I wonder if there's a merit badge for that?"

Of course there wasn't, but on a warm night later that summer, we sure could have used one. It might have kept us out of jail.

Two policemen on patrol that night saw movement in the back of an automobile dealership that was supposed to have been empty. They stopped their patrol car and decided to investigate. Drawing their guns, they separated, each one walking along a different side of the auto agency.

Nearing the back, one officer heard a voice say, "Drop your gun, Eddy."

He then heard a voice reply, "No, drop your gun, Bob."

A shot rang out. The policeman saw his partner stagger and fall backward. He was dead. Instead of rushing to apprehend the killer, the officer panicked and ran. He jumped over a fence and dropped about twelve feet to a side hill below the parking lot. The killers fled and got away.

When a policeman is killed in the line of duty, a shock wave goes through the entire community.

"Cop killer!" were the words coming from everyone's lips.

Petoskey's city officials reacted to the horrendous crime that had been committed. They petitioned the governor's office for help. The governor gave it. Eight hundred law officers descended upon the city of Petoskey. State police, sheriff's officers, U.S. marshals, and patrolmen from anywhere and everywhere were called upon. In fact, anyone with a badge who could possibly be spared came to help catch the despised murderers.

One of the largest manhunts in the state was soon under way. Unfortunately, the participants' zeal soon overtook their reasoning. They rushed down Main Street, grabbing every Indian in sight. They put them in police cars and took them to jail. Then they went to all the Indian homes, dragged the male folk out, and took them to jail. In a couple hours, there wasn't an Indian man left in the entire area.

Petoskey had two jails. The city jail was located in the basement of the courthouse. An impressive three-story building, the courthouse was located in the center of town and had a large four-faced clock in its tower. Under normal circumstances those with excessive drinking behavior or disruptive conduct occupied the city jail. When someone reappeared after an unexplained absence of a few days and was asked, "Where've you been?" the phrase "under the clock" explained everything.

During this manhunt, however, that phrase took on a very different meaning. The cops cleared out the city cells' normal occupants to make room for the large number of "suspects" being rounded up. Before long the cells were overflowing. That didn't slow the roundup down one bit. The county jail located across the street was cleared, and more "suspects" began filling those cells. Soon Petoskey's Indian men and many Indian boys were packed like sardines into both floors of the county jail.

Indians who'd never been in jail in their lives were rounded up and put behind those steel doors. Eighty-year-old Ike Naska, my mother's uncle, was thrown into jail so fast the law officers didn't realize his dog had run in with him. Those lawmen kept bringing in more and more Indians until the jails simply couldn't hold anymore.

Russ Johnson tried to slow and even stop the mad roundup.

"You're all wrong," he told them. "When you catch these killers, they won't be Indian. I've known these people all my life, and I don't believe for one minute that any of these men would do this kind of thing. This is just plain foolishness."

His voice was only one among the many. In all the uproar, it was easily ignored. Two days later, a man phoned the police.

"Two strange men just went into my barn," he told the officer answering the call. "I don't have the first idea who they are. I just know they don't have any business being in there."

"Don't do a thing," the sergeant warned him. "We'll be out to investigate immediately. Get your family and stay inside your house until we give you the 'all clear' sign."

The man agreed to do as he was told. The lawmen sprang into action. They surrounded the farmer's barn. Next they picked a team to rush the barn and try to force the strangers to surrender. The team stormed the barn with weapons drawn. No gunfire was exchanged. The two men were cowering in a horse stall. The manhunt had finally come to an end. The dreaded "cop killers" had been found.

The two men were brothers-in-law. They were white, upper-middle-class locals who lived on Pill Hill. As it turned out, the identity of the triggerman had been known all along. He and the dead patrolman had called each other by name. Whether it was his panic or just a certain mindset about who might commit such a crime that caused the dead patrolman's partner not to connect up the name he heard with a face, we'll never know.

Russ Johnson's words had come true: "When you catch these killers, they won't be Indians."

To his credit, the cop did testify against the men at their trial. Unfortunately for the Indians, finding the truth was not enough to change the deeply ingrained mindset that had caused the massive roundup. The two jails, full of Indians and one dog, were emptied. Were the police who had locked them up sorry? Was an apology forthcoming? No.

Instead, the big steel doors were thrown open and the air was filled with the surly words "Get out!"

Eighty-year-old Ike Naska was so upset by being accused of murder, he hitchhiked to neighboring Charlevoix to stay with other Indians. We finally had to go get him and assure him the real killers had been found.

These are the kinds of harassment Indian people had to endure. It sure made the words "you are just as good as anyone else" a little harder to believe.

· 23 ·

The Pranksters

Louie Adams's house sat on what we called "the Rim" in Hungry Hollow. Louie and Oakley passed many a summer evening in Louie's backyard watching the comings and goings of our little community and devising new ways for amusement. Needless to say, they had to find ways that didn't cost money or at least were very cheap. They got to be so good at it, they earned the reputation for being the best pranksters in all of Hungry Hollow.

Sheridan was just a narrow dirt road with one lonely streetlight on its west end. Cars were quite different then from those we see today. For one thing, their top speed was about 25 miles per hour. Louie's backyard was the perfect spot to watch each and every car and its occupants that drove by.

"Seems like everybody and their brother has driven by here tonight," Louie commented to Oakley one evening.

"Yea, even the mayor came by."

An idea popped into Oakley's head. Recognizing the look on his face, Louie immediately wanted to know, "What? Tell me. I'll bet it's a good one!"

Oakley didn't hesitate. "Well, we've sat here night after night, watching car after car drive by."

"Yah. So?"

"That's all that ever happens, right?"

"Yah. So?"

"So no one ever expects anything to happen when they drive down here, do they?"

"No, I guess not. What are you getting at?"

"Suppose we had a way to change all that. Suppose we had a way to make something happen when they least expected it?"

A big grin spread across Louie's face. "Then I suppose we'd have the makings of a pretty good prank! You got something in mind we could use to bring about this surprise?"

"The very thing," Oakley said. "Let's make a trip to the dump!"

Louie needed no further encouragement. They took off running.

"Ya mind telling me what we're looking for?" Louie asked when they reached the dump.

"Pasteboard."

"And just how is pasteboard going to surprise anyone?" Louie wanted to know.

"Well, it won't do much of anything until we turn it into a skeleton."

"What???? A skeleton! How the heck are we going to turn pasteboard into a skeleton?"

"We're not going to 'turn it into a skeleton,'" Oakley said. "If my idea works, it sure will look like one though."

Remembering Oakley's artistic skills, Louie started hunting for pasteboard. Before long, they had what they needed. Oakley then set about drawing and cutting and wiring things together. A life-size human skeleton soon lay on the ground before them. There was only one problem. It still looked like a cutout, pasteboard skeleton. They both knew it wouldn't scare anyone. This time Louie had an idea.

"Ya think silver paint might help this thing?" he wanted to know.

"As much as anything could." Oakley said. "Just where the heck are we going to get silver paint?"

Louie smiled. "I'll be right back."

After a few minutes, he returned with paint and brush in hand. Oakley burst out laughing. "I hope your father doesn't start to miss that."

Louie had purloined the silver paint from his contractor father. After the paint dried, they decided the skeleton was perfect for their intended prank. They laid it down in the middle of Sheridan Street. A cord fastened to the top of the skeleton was thrown up over the streetlight. Then they covered the skeleton with dirt so it couldn't be seen by approaching cars. Next, Louie and Oakley hid on the side of the road, waiting for a car to approach.

They didn't have to wait long. When the car was at the right distance, they pulled on the cord and the skeleton stood up in front of the car! The driver slammed on the brakes amid much cursing and yelling. What fun!! When the car drove away, the boys quickly covered the skeleton again and waited for their next victim.

The first few surprises went as expected. The boys were having a great time. Then, as is often the case in pranks, the unexpected happened. The tables were turned. A black car slowly came down Sheridan. At the right moment, the cord was pulled and the skeleton rose up and began dangling. The car came to a screeching halt. This time, however, the driver got out of his car. They saw him look around for the culprit of the prank. Fortunately, for Louie and Oakley, he failed to see them. Just when they were ready to breathe a sigh of relief, he walked up to the skeleton and yanked it from its cord. Skeleton in hand, he walked back to his car. He tossed their work of art into his backseat and drove off. The boys were speechless!

Oakley and Louie tried again. Another skeleton was created. After startling a few more cars, that skeleton was taken! When a fourth skeleton met with the same fate, that was more than they could take. It was just too much to have to keep making new skeletons. The game came to an end and the skeleton in the hollow went away forever. The same could not be said for the boys' pranks.

Louie Adams came up with the next one. Next to Lake Michigan, near the village of Bay Shore, stands a deserted lime kiln. Four of the old furnaces still stand to this day. These old kilns are three times the height of a man. Each has a catwalk ringing it about two-thirds of the way up toward its top. They stand amidst tumbled-down shacks and rusted pieces of tin roofs. In the moonlight, with the sound of waves breaking on the beach, these old kilns look ghostly.

Louie recruited Flop, Henry Dickerson, Archie Kiogima, and myself to help him execute his idea. He needed one body for each of the four kilns. As requested, we gathered at his house just after sundown. In the old car his dad used for painting jobs, he drove the four of us down through the woods, using the two-rut road to the old lime kiln. Even that much was "spooky" to me. Finally, he stopped the truck and shut off the engine. Louie pulled out a bottle of liquid white shoe polish from each of his two pockets. He handed one to me and the other to Archie.

"Smear this stuff all over your arms and faces," he instructed.

When we'd finished, we took a good look at each other. In the dim light, the others' faces looked like skulls to me, because we didn't paint close around our eyes.

"Now, I'm going back to get our victims," he said, smiling in anticipation. "Don't wait too long to get in place on the kilns," he added as he drove off.

Louie headed back to get a carload of girls. When we saw the car's lights coming down the road, we each scrambled up on one of the catwalks around the kilns. We lay down on the ledge, leaving just enough room to peer over it with our eyes. We could hear Louie and the girls laughing as he stopped the car about 20 yards from us. Louie had planned to tell ghost stories on the way down to the kiln.

We knew he'd set his plan in motion when one of the girls called out boldly, "I'm not afraid of ghosts."

"Give me that flashlight," she yelled.

She grabbed the light, turned it on, and came running toward us. She happened to pick the ledge I was lying on.

Darn! All this for nothing! She isn't even scared.

I was lying with my arms folded under my white face, looking down over the edge at her. I was grinning. She came running towards me with that flashlight pointing here and there. She stopped just below me and happened to shine that light right in my face. You've never heard such a scream! She threw the flashlight and ran stumbling and falling back to the truck. She was hysterical. Louie and the other girls tried everything to calm her down. Nothing worked. Finally, they drove off with her still screaming.

Bay Shore had a general store where the villagers hung around playing cards and checkers and socializing with one another. This is where Louie, claiming they needed help, took the girls. However, by the time they reached the general store, Louie was the only one begging for calm. There were several people gathered outside that night when Louie and his truckload of screaming girls pulled up. As you might imagine, this caused quite a commotion in the normally quiet and peaceful Bay Shore. All the people inside the store and others who were sitting around outside quickly jumped into their cars to go and see about these ghosts.

Back at the kilns, we watched Louie and the girls drive up the road and out of sight. When we were sure they were gone, we came down off the kilns.

"What did you do to that poor girl?" Archie wanted to know, laughing.

"I thought we were goners for sure. I'd no idea when she shined that light in my face it would scare her like that. I was smiling, though. Just like this," I said as I flashed Archie and the others a big smile.

They all burst out laughing.

"Too bad she got scared so soon," Flop added. "I had an even scarier look all ready for her."

He showed us what he meant. Again we burst out laughing. Next, Hank treated us to his look. And finally, Archie showed us his. We decided that as ghosts, we looked absolutely fiendish in the moonlight.

"What are we supposed to do now?" Archie wanted to know.

"Let's just wait 'til Louie comes back," I suggested.

All of a sudden, car lights appeared coming over the hill from Bay Shore. There were five cars in all. Each of them was loaded with mostly men and young boys, but there were also a few girls.

Flop yelled, "Get back on your kilns!"

We scrambled back to our places. The cars came to a stop and everyone unloaded. They started ghost hunting.

The first "ghost" they saw was Hank Dickerson on the farthest kiln.

"There it is. There it is!" they shouted.

The shouting was so loud it startled Hank, and he dropped back out of sight. A few of the cars had spotlights on them. Some of the ghost hunters started shining those spots towards the kilns. One of the spots caught Hank's stark white face in its glare. The sight of that stark white face in the moonlight, in the middle of the deserted lime kiln, was shocking to say the least. Archie was on the third kiln and was the next one to be caught in a spotlight.

Someone shouted, "That thing floated out over the lake and then landed up there!"

The shouts and exclamations told us the ghost hunters believed the ghost was on the move. These sightings of the "ghost" went on for about a half hour. Each time they caught one of us in their spotlights, the outcries continued. Luckily, they never spotted two of us at the same time. We hadn't planned it that way, it just happened.

Homer Willis, a young fellow who was in my class at school, suddenly got a shot of courage.

He loudly proclaimed, "I'm going up there and see what this is all about. I'm not scared!"

Homer decided to do his show of bravado on the kiln I was on. I heard him coming up the ramp and knew our game was soon to be over.

I'll just quietly tell Homer that it's only us having fun and to go back down among the crowd and tell them he saw nothing.

Homer slowly walked onto the catwalk until he got around to where I stood flattened against the wall of the kiln. When he was close enough, I stepped towards him with my arms outstretched to take hold of his coat. I only got one word out of my mouth.

"Homer," I whispered.

Startled, he yelled, "AWK!" and jumped backwards off the walk to the ground below.

In my haste to save our prank, I'd forgotten my arms and face were painted white. How it must have frightened him to see those white arms reaching towards him and to hear his name being called.

He ran back to the others more scared than I've ever seen anyone before or since. The ghost hunters gathered around him to hear what had happened.

"That does it!" one of them yelled. "I'm getting my rifle."

"Good idea!" someone else said.

"Let's go!"

With that, the ghost hunters headed for their cars. Not waiting to consult anyone, I scrambled down the back side of the kiln. I ran as fast as I could, hunched over, to the lake. I walked up the beach a ways before I stopped to wash off the shoe polish. Then I headed up to a place on the bluffs where Louie had told us to meet after the prank. I wasn't sure when or if I'd see the others that night.

I can always walk back home if I have to.

It wasn't long before the other three ex-ghosts showed up. They were just as anxious to get away from that place as I was. They, too, had heard the talk about getting guns. From where we were hidden in the woods, we could see the line of cars heading back up the road towards the village of Bay Shore. A half an hour later, Louie found us. He'd taken the girls home before returning to get us.

"Let's get out of here," he said.

Not one of us needed a second invitation to leave.

As we got into the truck, Archie spoke up, "Look! There are cars heading back towards the kiln."

"They're going back to investigate!" Flop exclaimed.

Louie added, "Maybe they have rifles, too!"

At school the next day, everyone was buzzing about the ghosts at the lime kiln. A large group was gathered around Homer. He was on crutches because he'd sprained his ankle when he leapt off the catwalk. Homer was telling them how he went face-to-face with the demon. He didn't mention that he'd yelled "AWK!"

"The strangest part of all," he said to his onlookers, "was that demon called me by name!"

Those standing around him gasped in horror.

"It was the most frightening thing I've ever seen," he went on. "That thing was huge. He stood ten feet tall if he stood an inch."

The crowd responded with more gasps. At this report, I could not help but smile to myself. Homer and I were exactly the same height.

Homer wasn't finished. "That thing had the foulest odor I have ever smelled. It was about like sulfur burning. Only much worse," he hastened to add.

Again I had to smile to myself. I didn't dare say anything to refute him. Everyone has an opinion about ghosts and goblins. Some people believe in them and some don't. After that night at the lime kiln, I'm sure the believers had a few more converts. We had no idea how powerful or long-lasting the results of our little prank would be. My daughter tells me that now, over fifty years later, they still talk about the haunting at the lime kiln.

· 24 ·

The Freight Train Killed Oakley

Folks called Oakley a bright, shining star. I believe that. Of course, no one is perfect. Oakley had his faults, but he never closed his eyes to them, and he would readily own up to each and every one.

"Bill," he'd say to me, "the best way to walk through life is with your eyes wide open."

I knew he was right, but I stumbled a lot trying to follow his advice. Whenever that happened, he was always the first one to extend his hand to help me back up.

"Take it easy, Bill," he'd say, with a smile that eased my pain. "We all stumble. That's just part of life. The important thing is to brush yourself off and move on."

The last time Oakley stumbled, I fell too. Harder and deeper than I ever had before. Only this time there was no Oakley to help me back up. That day changed my life and Hungry Hollow forever.

It started out like any other. I spent the morning doing the small things that are necessary in life but never worth noting. When I sat down to dinner, a vague feeling of dread came over me. It got stronger and stronger as the day wore on. The trouble was, I couldn't identify its source. I tried everything I knew to shake it off, but nothing worked. I even mentioned it to my brother. To my surprise, he told me he'd been feeling the same way. That was no help. I'll be darned if that feeling didn't follow me to bed that night, keeping me from falling asleep. I tossed and turned and tossed again, but sleep just would not come. Frustrated, I decided to read. Time and time again I had to bring my attention back to the same paragraph or word I'd just read. If I did manage to get through a sentence or two, I couldn't hold onto its meaning to save my soul.

Loud voices coming from down the hollow broke through my misery. I listened and realized they were getting louder and closer.

When I got up to investigate, I stepped into the worst nightmare of my life. From my window, I could see the lights coming on, door by door. Melvin Stowe came into view, and my feelings of dread took root.

In Hungry Hollow, we shared everything, including our reactions to big news when we heard it. All the shouting and commotion meant this was news of great magnitude.

My mother called out to me, "What is it?"

"It's Melvin, and he's going to every door all the way up the hollow."

The shuffling and ruffling sounds told me my parents were hurrying to get out of bed.

When Melvin turned into our yard, I was already standing in our doorway.

"It's Oakley!" he said between deep breaths. "He's dead! The freight train killed Oakley! He was your relative, wasn't he?"

Melvin's words ripped through me like a tornado, leaving my insides all jumbled up. I was unable to think or speak.

I turned when I heard my mother's loud gasp. My dad's arms were around her shoulders, trying to steady her. It was through her side of the family that we were cousins to Oakley.

"Bill! Bill!" Melvin was trying to get my attention. "Can you get me that water I asked for?"

I fumbled my way to our kitchen to grant his request.

I handed him the water, and after a quick drink he said, "I'm so sorry about Oakley. It's hard to believe. That kid was something special. We're all going to miss him."

He gulped down the rest of the water and went to finish his run up through the hollow.

Shock and grief do strange things to people and time. I was in our front yard for what seemed like hours, watching the lights come on in house after house as the news spread. In reality, only a few minutes had passed. Melvin's voice filled my ears, but my mind shut out his words. People soon began showing up at our house. I greeted each visitor and tried to make eye contact. No one had to tell me how much they liked Oakley or how much they'd miss him. Their eyes said it all. After awhile, I quit looking. I had to. I couldn't stand to see anymore of their pain. I didn't have the slightest notion how I was going to stand my own. Over and over, people kept asking one thing.

"What happened?"

Over and over, we'd tell them we didn't know. No one had any answers. A thick blanket of shock and grief descended upon Hungry Hollow that night. Everyone could feel it, but no one wanted to talk about it. What would have been the point? Not one of us could say for sure when or if it would lift.

The next morning, my dad and I went to Stone's Funeral Home to see what we could find out. Many Indians were already there, but they didn't know any more than we did.

My dad and I asked to meet with the funeral home director. We sat down to wait for him. After a few minutes, a well-dressed, somber-looking man appeared.

"I understand you are related to Oakley?"

"Yes, through my wife's side. Oakley was her nephew," my dad told him. "We're hoping we can find out what happened. It won't bring him back, but knowing might help us get through this."

The man looked at us for a few seconds and then said, "I'm not sure how much help I can be to you, but I'll do what I can."

He motioned for us to follow him as he led us into a small room that served as both a consulting room and office. There was a small settee with two matching easy chairs on either side. A desk sat in front of the small furniture grouping.

"Please, have a seat," he said as he made his way behind his desk to sit down.

Several folders lay in front of him. He shuffled through them until he found the one pertaining to Oakley. He leaned back in his chair and began reading. Several minutes later, he closed the folder and put it on top of the others.

"Perhaps the best way to handle this would be to start with what you do know," he said, looking directly at my father.

My father cleared his throat. "Late last night we were told Oakley was killed by a freight train. That's the long and the short of it."

My father was not one to mince words.

"What we'd like to find out is the how and the why of it, if possible."

"I see. I'm afraid I don't have those answers to give you. I can tell you he was killed down in the switching yards. The exact details are unclear as I understand them."

My father nodded.

The director continued. "You realize, since the young man's burial cost is coming from the state, there may not ever be more details."

He didn't have to go into the meaning behind his words. We knew autopsies weren't done on indigent people. The state of Michigan paid a very small fee to bury such people. It was only enough to get them underground. He'd just told us this would be Oakley's fate.

"Well, thank you for seeing us," my father said as he rose to his feet.

"I'm sorry I couldn't have been more help to you."

The director got up from his chair and started around his desk but my father stopped him.

"No, no," my father said, gesturing for him to stay put. "I can see you're a busy man, and we've troubled you enough. We can find our own way out."

With that we opened the office door and left.

"I am sorry for your loss," the director called out as we made our way down the hall.

Once outside, my father took a deep breath.

"Let's go see Russ Johnson."

We walked towards the police station in silence. My mind kept taking me to the switching yards. I couldn't begin to count the number of times Oakley and I and our other chums had been there. The yards were where the trains were "made up" and contained as many as a dozen sets of track. Switch engines ran constantly around town, taking freight cars to many different companies located here, there, and everywhere. If we were downtown and were going to the hollow, many of us—men, boys, and even some of the more daring girls—just went to the railroad tracks and waited for the next "switcher." Pictures of Oakley and many others running a few steps and then grabbing onto the rungs of the ladder that was always on a boxcar flooded my thoughts. How many times had we ridden with our feet on the bottom step while hanging onto the ladder? There I could feel the wind on my face and see trees and houses flashing by. Sheridan Street was never very far when you were riding the rails. As soon as she got in sight, you only had to step off and trot the few steps it took to regain your balance. There you were, and you'd saved yourself a mile-and-a-half walk.

The numerous warnings of the dangers involved came crashing into my mind now, too. How many times had we ignored those warnings, using those famous last words "everybody's doing it"? Those words were still true, but I'd never before weighed the real cost behind them. "Everybody" was now Oakley. Oakley of all people! He'd been one of the best. How could this have happened to him? I was the one it should have happened to. I was far less skilled and much more careless. I'd often mistaken a hot-shot freight train for a switcher. Oakley was the one to warn me time and time again to check the engine before hopping on.

"What's it going to take to get your attention, Bill?" he'd ask.

I never had an answer.

A hot-shot freight train looked just like a switcher if you didn't see the engine. The engine on the switchers were much smaller, with just two driving wheels on each side, while the bigger, long-distance freight trains had four or five driving wheels on each side. The first time I'd made that mistake came roaring into my head.

I'd been in a hurry to get home and grabbed the first train I saw heading toward the hollow. Unfortunately, I'd grabbed a long-distance freight-train instead of a local. I didn't realize it until I got to Sheridan Street and the train was going way too fast to get off.

More experienced freight-train hitchhikers could tell the difference much sooner. If they found they'd mistakenly gotten a "hot-shot," they simply stepped off when the train began to pick up too much speed. The "greenhorns" would end up 15 miles out in the country, going up a steep grade called Elmira. That was the first place the train slowed down enough to hop off.

My 15-mile walk back to Sheridan Street was long and hot. I was never so glad to see familiar territory in my life. When I finally spotted our house, there was Oakley sitting on our front step. He grinned at me as only Oakley could.

Instantly, I knew two things. First, he was glad to see me. And second, he'd warned me to be careful around those trains because everyone starts out as a greenhorn. He got up and walked to meet me.

"You made pretty good time, Bill" was all he said.

Remembering his smile now brought a big lump to my throat. I swallowed back my tears and took a deep breath. We were at the police station.

I followed my father up to the chief of police's desk.

"We'd like to speak to Russ Johnson if we can."

The sergeant looked up from his work and said, "He's out on a call. You can sit over there if you've a mind to wait for him."

My father and I sat down. It wasn't long before Russ returned.

"We've come to find out what we can about Oakley."

Russ nodded his head in understanding. "Let's step outside. I think we can talk better out there."

Once outside, he continued. "It's a real shame about Oakley. He was a fine young man. I can't tell you exactly what happened, because I didn't see it. I got there shortly afterwards, though."

"Whatever you can tell us would help," my father told him.

"I talked to several people who were there and could have seen what happened. From what I can piece together, Oakley simply stumbled and fell under the wheels of the train. I'm sad to say it tore him to pieces. One of the worst sights I've ever seen. As tore up as he was, I have to believe he went instantly. I expect there'll be no choice but to have a closed casket."

"We appreciate your time" was all my father could get out.

"It was no problem. Folks around here are going to miss him. He was a fine young man."

Then he added, "I wish there was something I could have done to help him. Anything."

There was nothing left for us to do but return home. The next few days passed in a blur of activity and emotion. We heard different stories of what'd happened. Some said Oakley had been drinking and that that was what'd caused him to stumble. I knew better. We were as close as two people can get, and I never saw him take that first drink. Others confirmed what Russ Johnson had told us. One thing was certain. All that talk did nothing to fill the hole Oakley's death left.

The walk to Oakley's funeral was one of the longest of my life. A part of me couldn't wait for the ceremony to be over, while another part wanted it to never begin. I longed to be free of all the pain I felt without ever having to say good-bye. I had to force myself to go inside the funeral home. I knew all too well Oakley was dead, but I wasn't prepared for the shock that went through me when I saw his casket.

As it turned out, Russ Johnson was wrong about it being closed. Jennie White, a distant cousin of Oakley, took a fine drape to the funeral home. They used it to drape him in a **V** shape. The drape showed only his head and a little of his chest.

It took every ounce of my strength to walk up to his casket and look inside. To my great relief, Oakley had a real peaceful look on his face. His look gave me more comfort and reassurance than all the words I heard that day put together. Even in his death, Oakley was still trying to take care of me.

It was like he was standing right beside me saying, *See Bill. You're stronger than you think. Don't you worry about me. I'll never be more than a thought away from you. And I'll be waiting for you when your walk is done. Now go on and make your life a good one. You deserve it. Don't ever forget that.*

I was glad his casket was open. Saying good-bye is a whole lot easier when you can see who you're saying it to.

To no one's surprise, it was a big funeral. I couldn't get over how many different kinds of people Oakley's death brought together.

John Foley was there. He's the one who gave Oakley the set of artist's supplies. Mrs. Pailthorpe came, too. She was the art teacher who said she taught Oakley everything he knew. She was also the one who changed the eyes on Oakley's painting *The White Stag*.

The mayor came to pay his respects but couldn't stay for the funeral. Farmer Thompson came and brought his wife. Michigan Maple Company sent someone to represent them. I didn't catch his name, though. Wayne Chamberlain came and represented the Kiwanis club. Of course there were lots of Indians there, too. All the elders came. Since Oakley was as handsome as a movie star, no one was surprised to see two Indian girlfriends crying their eyes out for him.

Oakley's funeral did hold one surprise for us Indians. A very pretty white girl came and sat in the back row. She couldn't hide her grief. None of us knew anything about her. All we did know was that most white people usually didn't have much to do with Indians.

The thing I remember most about the funeral itself is the eulogy. The preacher said Oakley had so many talents we would never know what he might have done in life had he not been killed. He said he was one of the bright, shining stars of Hungry Hollow.

I felt honored to be a pallbearer. All six of us wore our Boy Scout uniforms. It turned out to be a good thing, because not one of us owned a regular suit.

After the funeral, I went to the bluff where Oakley had painted the $25 picture of Petoskey's beautiful sunset. I felt a deep emptiness. I always knew good things happened when Oakley was around. I thought that was why he was so popular. That day, as I looked out over the bay and remembered all the good times we'd shared, I realized I'd been wrong. It wasn't the good things that happened when Oakley was around that brought everyone to that funeral. Oakley walked through life with his eyes open. The difference between him and most folks was he kept his eyes open wide enough to see around a person's faults and find the best of who they were. Once he found it, he never lost sight of it. When someone stays focused on that part of you, it's easier for that part to show up to face a problem or have a discussion. Under those conditions, good things and good feelings almost always follow. That's what really made Oakley a bright, shining star. How he knew to do that, I'll never know. I'm just glad he did.

People don't get over losing someone they love. They do learn how to move on, because life does. It takes time. It did after Oakley died. Plenty of it.

· 25 ·

The Day I Stopped
Killing Animals

I saw her running at a lope along the side of a hill. I knew she would pass in an opening about 50 yards downhill from me. I clicked off the safety and raised the .30–30 rifle towards the opening in the trees. When she came into the clearing, I pressed the trigger. The rifle bucked against my shoulder. I heard the shot go reverberating across the hills and vales.

The big doe deer immediately fell and slid 15 yards in the snow. I did not see the fawn on the other side of the doe. The bullet went right through the doe and took the jaw off the fawn. The doe had kept going until the severity of her wound brought her down. She frantically raised her head as if to communicate with her offspring for as long as possible. Her breathing was labored. Her half-opened eyes split their attention between searching the countryside for danger and the tiny fawn at her side. Bright red blood soaked the stark white snow as the doe quietly slipped into the beyond. The rest of the herd had gone, leaving the sad duo to face the inevitable.

In that moment, the enormity of what I'd done struck me. I began to tremble. I had to force myself to be calm. I pumped another shell into the chamber of the .30–30, put the front sight on the little deer's ear. I dropped the sight to the middle of its head and pressed the trigger again. The shot rang out and the little fellow dropped over. He was dead when he hit the ground. His suffering was over. Mine was just beginning.

I hunkered down in a squat and leaned against a tree. My tears blinded me, and I fervently prayed, *Forgive me God, for what I have done to two of your creatures.*

That morning my father told Flop and me as we left the house, "Get any kind of game. Hungry Hollow needs meat."

That was my reason for killing the doe and her fawn. Hungry Hollow Indians, old and young, got the meat. As for me, I would have none of it.

When we got home that evening, I didn't go into our house right away. I sat out on the front porch and planned as best I could what I would say. I'd never spoken to my dad in a contrary manner. It wasn't an easy thing to even think about, let alone do. I loved my father. That was it in a nutshell. Plain and simple.

Finally, I could put it off no longer. I went in and walked over to my father, who was sitting in his rocking easy chair.

I laid the rifle in his lap and said, "I'm through with it. Don't ever ask me again to go killing animals with you or for you."

I'd expected an outburst. It didn't happen.

He merely nodded his head and said, "Hand me the cleaning kit."

He set about cleaning the .30–30 rifle. When he was finished, he hung it on the gun rack. He never invited or asked me to go hunting again.

Fifty years have passed since that time. I've never had that first regret about my decision.

When I hear hunters call killing animals "sport," I say, "When the animals learn to shoot back, maybe I, too, will call it 'sport.'"

· 26 ·

War!

The clouds of war were gathering. They had been for some time. We tried to ignore them, hoping like everyone else that they would go away.

They didn't. The powerful and mad men over the big salty water wouldn't let them go away. One day old Ellory came through hollering that the Italians were fighting Italy! Some snickered, but Ellory's voice was dead serious. We'd already heard about Italy invading Ethiopia, so we knew what he meant.

Over the next few years we began to hear words like Hirohito, Tojo, and Goering. News of places that meant nothing to us before, like Pearl Harbor, Midway, and Guam, filled the radio airways. One day, Melvin Stowe, the news spreader, came running up through the hollow. We could hear him yelling way down the line.

Long before he reached us, my dad said, "We're at war."

People everywhere were saying it was sneaky little yellow men who had attacked our bases at Pearl Harbor. They'd attacked without even declaring war.

By the time I got to the haircutting place to listen to the news on the radio, the place was wall-to-wall with Indians. Even more Indians were standing outside, trying to hear the news. President Roosevelt was addressing the nation. No one said a word as we listened to him tell us that "the day of infamy" had arrived. Most of us were too stunned to speak. Some of the women were crying. They released their feelings quicker than the men and boys in the crowd. Everyone knew many of us would be marching away to be killed or to have their arms and legs shot off.

Just a few minutes after the president finished speaking, Frank Greenleaf turned off the radio and the arguments began.

Some Indians said, "Why should we go away and fight to the death for a country that has already been taken away from us?"

Another said, "Go home and watch your kids eat fish-head soup and pancakes while the kids up on Pill Hill eat pork chops, steak, and ice cream. Then ask yourself if you're willing to die for that!"

Still another Indian volunteered, "I heard two men down at the courthouse say, 'The only good Indian is a dead Indian.' This was just yesterday."

Momentum against fighting for this country was growing fast among the young Indians of Hungry Hollow. Who could blame them? Most of them could remember more abuse than praise. They'd been called dirty names by people they didn't even know. They'd been refused work and a chance to earn food for their families, when they could plainly see work was there for the men of the right skin color. They'd been first to be accused when a crime was committed anywhere in the area.

George Waboose, "the Rabbit," shouted, "We're fourth-class in our own country!"

Then Leo Meshekey, "the Turtle," yelled out, "Let's all go home and think it over. We'll meet again."

The crowd of Indians broke up and walked away still grumbling. All over Hungry Hollow, little groups gathered here and there to talk things over. About a week after Roosevelt's speech, the Indians gathered again. I ran to get my father. We all went down to the Greenleafs' to listen.

Leo Meshekey was just beginning to speak when we arrived.

"Yes, our land has been torn from us. Yes, we've been starved, beaten up, and spit upon. In our own country, no one has been treated worse except maybe the black man. We've had to watch our hungry children wade through the snow with no coats and with holes in their shoes. We've had to send them to school without the proper clothing on their backs or without books to study from. I say you are right when I hear you talk of not shedding your blood in exchange for the indignities you've had to endure—indignities that were thrust upon you just because you happened to be born Indian.

"We no longer hold title to the land we stand on today. Hear me good, now. This land was given to us by Zhamadoo, the Creator. It was given to us to live on and love while always bearing in mind that the earth is our mother. The hairy men from the east came here from the land given to them by the Creator and tore this land from us. They used lying tongues and clever weapons of war to do it. These facts I do not dispute.

"I say to you today, this land still belongs to the Creator. In the eyes of the Creator, the white man's actions and papers find no recognition. For all that has happened, this land is no less our homeland than when the Creator first placed us upon it. This part of the earth is still our mother. What manner of children would we be if we refused her protection? I, for one, will fight to protect our mother until the last breath leaves my body. I, for one, will fight side by side with those who have robbed us and even raped our womenfolk. I do not have any reason to consider these men worth dying for. But I tell you this. There are even worse men to the east and west of us. Depraved men who would look upon us with the same eyes as the white men who plundered us. I tell you these are men who would dehumanize us more than do these pillagers who now rule. Men who would destroy our Mother Earth's protectors without so much as one blink of an eye."

I watched the Turtle's words take hold of all who listened. I saw their faces light up as the reality of their situation became clear to them.

Shouts like "He's right!" "Hear the Turtle!" and "Protect our Mother Earth!" went up loud and long.

Many of these Indians of the right age and of sound body went immediately and joined the armed force of their choice. Indians always distinguished themselves in battle. That is a fact. No man can take that away from them. My dad, who was in the Spanish-American War, said it. My uncle, who was gassed in World War I, said it was true of his war. And this war, soon to be dubbed World War II, was no different.

We watched many of the Indian boys and men march away

with holes in their shoes and patches on the seat of their pants. I was only sixteen, but I decided I needed to be among them. Many would not return. They would have given their lives for the ideas the Turtle had inspired in their hearts. Many of those who came marching back home did so resplendent in their uniforms and covered with medals. Many of these brave men are now dead and gone.

I was told by some of the survivors, "They didn't boast of their deeds while they were alive, so don't write of them now, Bill. That was the way they would have wanted it."

I'll not name them, but I won't close this subject without telling you many brave men did not return from the war. Of those who did return, the medals pinned to their uniforms said it all.